Here's what reviewers are saying about this book—

"Dr. Macky has rendered a service to the educated layman who wants a succinct survey of modern biblical problems. Without being superficial, this masterly guide leads the reader through books of the Bible but pauses meaningfully on the topics of Christian faith, fundamentalism, and mythical language. The value of the book lies in its intelligible explanation of the complex methodology of biblical interpretation. In an atmosphere of ecumenism, this competent author moves easily from literary and historical problems to theological teachings. Dr. Macky couches his learning in informative and gripping examples which make his book one of the most readable of its kind. This unique primer should be in the hands of all who are beginning or reviewing a general course on the Bible."—The Reverend Joseph A. Grispino, S.M., Assistant Professor of Sacred Scripture, Department of Theology, Loyola University of Los Angeles.

"This disarming little volume covers many complex and controversial issues clearly, rationally, and cogently. Using simple language and down-to-earth illustrations, Macky deals with such issues as the authority of the Scriptures, the origin and boundaries of the canon, demythologizing, and the significance of various critical approaches to the study of the Bible. This bridge between the scholar and the layman is thought-provoking for the complacent, and most sustaining for the frustrated inquirer. Macky's Christian commitment is clear, but it is indicated in lively and open discussion rather than weighty and restrictive credo."—John B. Trotti, *Library Journal*.

"Those conversant with current textual studies and theological emphases will appreciate that the author is fully at home in these areas. He writes as one who knows the game and knows the score. The parish pastor who also knows his way through these same problematic areas will appreciate that the author has dared to state the inevitable conclusions without in any way detracting from the central core of the Gospel. Laymen informed in the fields of literary criticism will appreciate the resounding faith affirmations that are really strengthened rather than weakened by the author's courage to ask and attempt to answer many of the tough questions concerning the Bible. The God of whom it speaks is still active, still engaging men in dialogue about the fundamental issues of life."—Arnold E. Carlson, *Lutheran Forum*.

"One could hardly find a better book for generating excitement in the classroom or in discussion groups."—Virginia Mollenkott, William Paterson College of New Jersey.

"If you are one of those who desires to deepen your faith and understanding, then this book is well worth your reading. But if not—if you have no desire to deepen your faith and understand the implications of it—then read something else."—Pastor Richard L. Dosh, *The Church Advocate*.

"Here is another treasure for the inquiring soul who is eager to enlarge upon his own interpretation of the Bible. . . . The book is a sharp, clinical study and would make an excellent springboard for discussion among those seeking more meaningful reading of the perennial best seller."—Jessie McCullough, *Denver* (Colo.) *Post*.

The Bible in Dialogue With Modern Man

by

Peter W. Macky

WORD BOOKS, Publisher
Waco, Texas

THE BIBLE IN DIALOGUE WITH MODERN MAN *by Peter W. Macky.* Copyright © 1970 *by Word, Incorporated, Waco, Texas. Printed in the United States of America. All rights reserved. No part of this book may be used or reproduced in any manner without written permission except in the case of brief quotations in critical articles and reviews. For information write Word Books, Publisher, 4800 West Waco Drive, Waco, Texas 76710.*

ISBN 0-87680-828-3
LIBRARY OF CONGRESS CATALOG CARD NUMBER: 74-96288

FIRST PRINTING JANUARY 1970
FIRST PAPERBACK PRINTING NOVEMBER 1976

To Nancy

Preface

A visitor feels lost the first time he walks into the ancient Bodleian Library in Oxford. He needs someone to show him around. The library is divided into several different buildings, each with its own obscure entrance. To make matters worse, the interiors of these ancient buildings are so filled with odd corners, long halls and dead-ends that a guide or a map is essential for finding books.

The Bible is likewise an ancient library that no man can rightly understand simply by walking in its front door and looking around. Two thousand years of dispute and discussion have made it clear that the rooms in this library must be labelled, and guides must be stationed along the way to help the uninitiated traveller get the most out of his journey through the biblical library.

This book is an attempt at labelling and guiding. It is written for those who have some knowledge already of the stories and thought of the Bible but do not know how to grasp what the whole Bible really means.

The questions that are considered in the three sections of the book are: Where is the authority of the Bible centered? What value is there in literary and historical criticism? What is the central theological thrust of the Bible? An introduction to these questions is supplied so that the reader may decide for himself what seems to be the right approach. "What does the Bible really say to us today?" Bible readers ask. The aim

Preface

of this book is to take readers along the paths trod through the biblical library in search of its deepest meaning.

The chapters that comprise this book were originally written as weekly lessons for the Lay Academy of the Pacific Palisades Presbyterian Church. The thoughts and comments of the participants helped to clarify difficulties and emphasize what was meaningful, and so, many thanks are due those who took part.

Others read the original version also and offered helpful comments. In particular I would like to thank Prof. Daniel Migliore of Princeton Theological Seminary who offered many very instructive comments on the last four chapters.

Finally, I want to thank my wife, Nancy, who read and re-read, discussed and re-discussed, typed and re-typed until these thoughts came to be almost as much hers as mine.

CONTENTS

1. CHRISTIAN FAITH AND THE OLD TESTAMENT   17
2. NEW TESTAMENT CLAIMS TO AUTHORITY   38
3. THE CHURCH'S ANCIENT LIBRARY   60
4. THE INERRANT BIBLE OF FUNDAMENTALISM   85
5. THE LITERATURE OF THE BIBLE   108
6. GOD'S HISTORY BOOK   131
7. THE HISTORY OF GOD'S ACTS   153
8. THE MYTHICAL LANGUAGE OF THE BIBLE   177
9. BIBLICAL INTERPRETATION TODAY   199

Introduction

The Bible stands in a paradoxical position today. On the one hand, it is not as widely known or influential as it has been during the past four centuries. One can no longer assume its contents, imagery, and language are familiar to the educated man. On the other hand, the status of biblical studies has seldom been as flourishing as it is today. Textual scholars have produced more accurate texts than hitherto have been available, translations abound in virtually every language and idiom, ecumenical collaboration among Roman Catholics, Orthodox, and Protestants extends to joint versions and commentaries, and biblical theology and hermeneutics are capturing the interest and enthusiasm of today's student generation.

Perhaps the explanation of this paradox is to be found in the rapidly changing character of American Christianity. Its old patterns were largely frontier in origin, and its view of the Scriptures was too often formal and legalistic. The Bible was regarded as a "sacred book," an authoritarian standard rather than a source of meaning and a means of grace. Now a deeper and freer relationship with the Bible is developing, and out of this has come a new sense of its nearness and relevance to the modern situation. It is not uncommon to find study groups on Old and New Testament themes or classes in Old and New Testament books bringing to bear biblical insights on the burning issues of today, or to find interpreters like Moltmann describing the present situation in terms of the Exodus, and the Church as the pilgrim people of God.

There is mounting evidence that a revival of interest in biblical studies is taking place in other lands. In totalitarian countries, where travel is banned or severely restricted and where relations with other churches are minimal or nonexistent, one often hears from Christians that they feel closer to the New Testament Church than to any other body however contemporaneous. Conditions have driven them back to the Scriptures, and they have found a kinship to the Apostolic commuities that enables them to understand their own situation and to find in the Lord of the Church the resources not only for survival but for effective witness. Many of the churches in the young African nations tell the same story, except in a different context. Suspicious of foreign ideology, even the ideology contained in translations and other forms of the Church's tradition, they have turned to the Bible itself and have found an affinity with the New Testament Church that is closer than any they share with contemporary churches in other cultures. And one need only mention the experience of the American black churchmen, who are finding in the Old Testament the motifs of liberation, restitution, and justice that speak most directly to the condition of their people.

It is precisely because of this new situation in America and in other lands that there is a new readiness to read and hear the Bible on its own terms, freed from alien doctrines and theories. But to be able to do this intelligently requires some background and understanding of the Bible's character, history, and how it has fared in the hands of its interpreters across the centuries. Hence the timeliness of Dr. Macky's volume. It is not dogmatic nor does it attempt to steer the reader along some predetermined path through the books of the Bible. It is, as the title suggests, a book to be read with profit by any intelligent person who would approach the Bible with the requisite understanding to be able to hear its message in all its liveliness and contemporaneity.

This is not to say that Dr. Macky has no point of view or

Introduction

convictions of his own. Clearly for him the Bible is a Christian book, and Jesus Christ is the Lord of the Scriptures. Thus the Old Testament is understood as no longer standing on its own feet but as a signpost pointing to Christ. The key question of authority is also answered in terms of the supreme authority of Jesus Christ, and the Resurrection is seen as the very heart of biblical faith.

Dr. Macky includes in his volume a discussion of a wide range of topics, such as the canon, the historical, literary, and theological nature of the Bible, and modern trends in biblical scholarship. Especially illuminating are accounts of the new hermeneutic, a critical appraisal of the demythologizing work of Bultmann, the new quest for the historical Jesus, and the theology of hope. Throughout the several chapters the author's style is simple and clear, his spirit is critical but reverent, and he proves himself to be an engaging and reliable cicerone with the natural gifts of a sensitive and able teacher. One may safely predict that the readers of this volume will be in a better position to hear more faithfully through the pages of the Old and New Testaments what the Spirit is saying to the churches today.

James I. McCord, President
Princeton Theological Seminary

The Bible in Dialogue with Modern Man

1

Christian Faith and the Old Testament

What did Jesus think of the Old Testament? The truth appears to be that He rejected its authority over Himself. Such a statement is shocking to many who have read the words of Jesus many times and understand Him to accept the Old Testament as if God Himself had spoken it. This latter interpretation is not overly surprising because Jesus' words are ambiguous: on the one hand He often opposes the Jewish Scripture as if it were inhuman, but He also often speaks about it in terms that any devout Jew would have applauded. How is this paradox to be explained? Seeking an answer to that question is the chief aim of this chapter. In order to see the issue clearly, statements of both viewpoints will be presented so that a judgment can be made with the evidence laid out before us. The evidence presented will come not only from the teaching of Jesus, but also from the rest of the New Testament, for the same paradox is found there.

THE MASTER'S VOICE

ETERNAL STANDARD

In much of His teaching, Jesus apparently accepted the authority of the Scriptures which had been handed down throughout the history of Israel. He often quoted them as the final authority. In the Temptation Narrative each of the

17

temptations was answered by, "It is written," followed by a quotation from the book of Deuteronomy. He answered the final temptation by saying, "Begone, Satan! for it is written, 'You shall worship the Lord your God and Him only shall you serve' " (Matt. 4:10).

"It is written" is like Billy Graham saying, "The Bible says," or the advertising agent for a national magazine saying, "I read it in *Newsweek*." Quoting an authority means, "I believe this source to be true." The difficult question that eventually needs to be answered is this: did Jesus look upon *all* parts of the Old Testament as worthy of quotation, or did He have standards by which He separated the wheat from the chaff? Only further evidence can determine this.

Not only did He quote the Old Testament, but Jesus also spoke of it as inspired by the Holy Spirit. The "Holy Spirit" means the active presence of God Himself. This is unlike our use of the word "spirit," for when we speak of "the spirit of Lincoln," we mean only the memory of his life and ideals and their continuing impact. Jesus' words were: "David himself, inspired by the Holy Spirit, declared, 'The Lord said to my Lord, Sit at my right hand, till I put your enemies under your feet' " (Mark 12:36). There is nothing in the Psalm from which this quotation is taken (Ps. 110) that indicates any special connection of the Holy Spirit with that Psalm. Since Jesus spoke this way of this Psalm, He may have thought that all of the Psalms and all of the Old Testament were inspired by the Holy Spirit. But that is not certain. Only this Psalm is mentioned. It could well have been the ambiguous use of the word "Lord" that made Jesus say that this particular saying was inspired by the Holy Spirit.

Dots and Bars

A far more important passage for our subject than any discussed so far is Matthew 5:17-19. "(17) Think not that I have come to abolish the law and the prophets; I have come not to abolish them but to fulfil them. (18) For truly, I say to you, till heaven and earth pass away, not an iota, not a dot, will pass from the law until all is accomplished. (19) Whoever then relaxes one of the least of these commandments and teaches men so, shall be called least in the kingdom of heaven; but he who does them and teaches them shall be called great in the kingdom of heaven." Here is an apparently uncompromising statement that the Old Testament (known as "the Law and the Prophets") is of eternal validity, that all the commandments in it, even the most horrifying (like stoning adulterers), are to be obeyed by Christians.

Taken by itself that is what it appears to mean. But can it be taken by itself? Are we not liable to distort a story if we read only the headlines and not the details which limit and explain the main point? In fact, a true understanding of this passage only comes by taking into consideration its context in the Sermon on the Mount, where (as we shall see) Jesus rejects several Old Testament laws by the contrast, "You have heard it said . . . but I say to you."

Several points must be noted if these verses are to be understood. The word "Law" to us means legally binding statutes, but to a Jew it was a broader term, for it meant the account of God's dealings with Israel, recorded in the Old Testament in the first five books, the Pentateuch. In verse 18 the word "Law" does not stand for the legal parts of the Old Testament, as we usually assume. Rather it is a short form, a poetic parallel, of the phrase in verse 17, "The law and the prophets," which means the whole of the Old Testament. The primary emphasis of verses 17 and 18 is not upon obedience to commandments. Instead it is upon "fulfillment" of the Law and the Prophets. Jesus emphasized the importance of the Old Testament as Promise, and His own ministry as Fulfillment of that Promise. To "fulfill" the Old Testament means to be the One towards Whom it pointed. We still use the phrase, "The fulfillment of men's hopes," as, Abraham Lincoln was the fulfillment of black men's hopes for an Emancipator.

Fulfillment

But fulfillment of promise is a very different point from the statement in verse 19 that all "these commandments" must be obeyed. In its present context this means "all the commandments of the Old Testament," which is certainly not Jesus' view, as innumerable statements to be presented below will attest. This means that verse 19, as Jesus meant it, will be better understood if it is removed from its context here.

Jesus was not emphasizing obedience to commandments in verses 17 and 18, and so verse 19 just does not belong here. If it is a saying of His, it probably referred to His own commandments, or to a limited group of Old Testament commandments.

This passage, in its first two verses, clearly emphasizes the authority of the Old Testament. The central issue of Matthew 5:17 is that Jesus came to fulfill the Old Testament, not to destroy it. Many times Jesus pointed to the Old Testament as a foreshadowing and promise of His own mission. Abolitionist literature in the 19th century was this same kind of foreshadowing and promise of freedom to the slaves.

According to Luke 4:16-21, Jesus came to His own home town synagogue and read a passage from Isaiah concerning God's Servant upon whom the Spirit of the Lord would descend. When He had finished reading, He announced "Today this promise has been fulfilled in your hearing," claiming that He was the Servant toward whom Isaiah had pointed.

Even more important in emphasizing Jesus' understanding of the Old Testament as God's promise are the Passion prophecies. Often when Jesus pointed ahead to His death, He pointed to "everything that is written of the Son of Man by the prophets" (Luke 18:31), implying that His life was determined by prophecies in the Old Testament: "For I tell you that this Scripture must be fulfilled in me, 'And He was reckoned with transgressors'; for what is written about me has its fulfillment" (Luke 22:37, see also Mark 14:49). Jesus apparently thought that the Old Testament pointed toward Him, and that His life and death would have to follow the course that God had laid down and revealed to the prophets. In a similar way Communists have followed the course laid out for them in Karl Marx's writing, for they believe him to be their authority who foresaw that captalism would eventually collapse.

It seems to be clear, therefore, that Jesus to some extent accepted the authority of the Old Testament. He quoted it to silence temptation, pointed to its commandments as part of the way to eternal life, claimed that the Holy Spirit inspired one of its writers, and claimed that it pointed toward Him and constrained Him in His actions. It is not unreasonable to conclude from this that Jesus thought that the Old Testament was of eternal validity, as most Jews of His time believed.

Yet even in discussion of passages that most strongly support the Old Testament there are signs that Jesus did not give it a blanket endorsement. His emphasis on the Old Testament as foreshadowing Him may indicate where He thought its continuing validity lay. His claim that He is the key to its true understanding may be the first sign of a standard by which He differentiated between the eternal and the temporal in the Old Testament. These hints can now be drawn out into forthright statements.

OUTMODED SYMBOL

In a considerable number of other passages Jesus did not accept the letter of the Old Testament as His authority. Indeed He rejected the explicit meaning of the law and set something else in its place. The question that we must face is this: what are the standards by which He judged between parts of the Old Testament? Was it simply His direct consciousness of God's will that led Him to substitute His word for the letter of the law? Or are there principles behind His teaching that can be discerned by reading closely?

The Old and the New

The most interesting changes that Jesus made in His disciples' understanding of the law are found in Matthew 5, the beginning of the Sermon on the Mount. In two instances Jesus extended the meaning of the law so that it included inward disposition as well as outward behavior. Anger is as bad as murder (5:22), lustful looks are adultery (5:28). The rest of the laws are reversed.

In the Old Testament law, divorce was allowed, but Jesus declared that this was not God's intention. Rather, He said, God proclaimed that husband and wife have become one person. Therefore, divorce, as the destruction of this new person, is adultery in God's eyes (Mark 10:2-12). Matthew 5:32 softens this hard saying by allowing divorce "on the ground of unchastity," thus saying that Jesus did not totally abrogate the Old Testament allowance of divorce, but simply defined it narrowly, in line with one of the Jewish schools of His time.

In Old Testament times swearing, making vows to God, was a regular part of Jewish worship (Deut. 23:21). Jesus declared that swearing should be completely avoided, because men should be so truthful that swearing is not needed (Matt. 5:34). We know what He meant. When a man today begins to swear by his sainted mother, we begin to be suspicious.

When a man committed a crime in ancient Israel, the law of retaliation was simple and clear: "An eye for an eye, a tooth for a tooth" (Ex. 21:23f). This was not only allowed, but was understood to be commanded by God. Jesus, however, declared that individuals must not follow that path if they are truly to be God's people: "But I say to you, Do not resist one who is evil. But if anyone strikes you on the right check, turn to him the other also" (Matt. 5:39). This saying was a complete revolution, for it proclaimed that retaliation itself was not really God's will, that reconciliation with the offender was God's cherished objective. This goes completely against a natural human instinct, which desires revenge, an instinct that was codified (and restricted) by the law of retaliation. Men today still exhibit belief in this law when they uphold capital punishment for murder. Jesus rejected this desire as sinful, and so rejected the law also, urging men to put it aside and love even those who abuse them.

Love, not War

He made this point even more clearly when He said: "You have heard that it was said, 'You shall love your neighbor and hate your enemy.' But I say to you, Love your enemies and pray for those who persecute you" (Matt. 5:43f.). The Law of Moses did not specifically order men to "hate their enemies," but all nations seem to honor this as one of their fundamental principles. The example of many Old Testament writers made this clear as a common way of life: "Do I not hate them that hate thee, O Lord? . . . I hate them with perfect hatred; I count them my enemies" (Ps. 139:21f.). This was especially the attitude of most Israelites· towards Gentiles. Several times we hear of complete massacres of Gentile cities by the Israelites (Josh. 6:21) under the belief that God called them to hate their enemies even to the point of destroying them completely, men, women, children, and animals. The extermination of the Jews by Hitler is the same kind of thing the early Israelites practiced. Jesus completely rejected that approach to life, standing firmly against that stream of Old Testament thought which asserted that God was a God of war who fought always on the side of Israel, urging her to destroy people who did not believe in Him.

This was not, of course, the main thrust of the Old Testament, for the prophets agreed far more with Jesus than with the "holy war" teaching of other parts of the Old Testament. What Jesus did was to affirm that the prophetic view was God's view, that love of enemies rather than hatred was the way men are called to live. Instead of "squeezing the Germans until the pips squeaked," which was Allied policy after World War

I, the approach of friendship and help after World War II was far closer to Jesus' urging.

Did Jesus think of the Old Testament passages that proclaim holy war and hatred of enemies? Did He think they simply were wrong and always had been, that man's natural instincts were being proclaimed as God's will? Or did He think that that was a necessary way of life for Israel when she was young? The most probable answer is that if hatred and war were wrong in AD 30 they must have been wrong in 1330 BC. Presumably, Jesus did not accept statements of Old Testament writers which claim that God demands slaughter of enemies.

People, not Religion

Jesus' most sweeping repudiation of Old Testament laws came in His dialogue with the Pharisees about eating with unwashed hands. The Old Testament did not specifically command that Jews wash before eating, but this was a "tradition of the elders" that the Pharisees thought ought to be imposed upon all the people. Jesus not only rejected that imposition but went even further. He widened the discussion to include all the eating laws of the Old Testament, which are numerous.

The principle that He presented is that "there is nothing outside a man which by going into him can defile him" (Mark 7:15). Quite the contrary, man is defiled by the things that come out of his heart: evil thoughts, pride, coveting, adultery, murder (7:21f.). The conclusion that Mark drew from this story, a conclusion that seems to be the intention of Jesus, was, "Thus he declared all foods clean" (7:19). That was a revolutionary saying also, for Leviticus 11 is filled with names of "unclean" animals which Jews were forbidden to eat, and Jesus said that such laws are of no importance. Instead, man's moral life, what comes out of his heart, is what counts. This is like telling a church member today, "It doesn't matter whether you go to church every Sunday or not; what matters is whether your daily life is loving."

The other central Jewish practice that Jesus rejected was, in fact, strict Sabbath observance. Many times He came into conflict with the Jewish leaders over this question. Several times He healed people on the Sabbath (Mark 3:1ff., Luke 14ff., John 9:16), thereby arousing the antagonism of His opponents, for He deliberately acted compassionately to teach the lesson that compassion comes before ritual. This same point, that human need takes precedence over religion, was made in the story of His disciples picking grain to eat on the Sabbath.

In this story Jesus went further than just saying human need in general took precedence over the Sabbath. He said in fact that He, "the Son of man, is lord of the Sabbath" (Mark 2:28).

Here again, as with the laws on revenge, love is His central standard. Man's greatest concern should be for what others need, and if they need it on the Sabbath, they should be given it, even if it entails work. The Jews had understood the Sabbath law as something holy that they were to serve. Jesus, on the other hand, understood it as an example of God's good gifts to men, relieving them from constant labor. The standard of action is therefore, what is good for other men, not what the law demands. So today the speed limit on our highways is rigidly enforced, but when it is a matter of life and death, the police will even escort us at high speed to get to the hospital. The law is made for man and is flexible in the light of man's needs.

From this description of Jesus' opposition to Old Testament laws, ideas, and interpretations, it seems clear that Jesus substantially repudiated the Old Testament. This conclusion must be balanced by the previous conclusion that in some way He also accepted it as authoritative. Exactly what His standards of interpretation were are not entirely clear, but some important points have come out. Before taking up the debate on how to combine these two tendencies, however, we must look into Paul's thought and that of the rest of the New Testament. Possibly, they will supply further clues to resolving the paradox of a repudiated yet authoritative Old Testament.

THE APOSTLE'S RESPONSE

ETERNAL PROCLAMATION

Paul's letters give evidence that he accepted the authority of the Old Testament in some of the same ways Jesus did. Paul quoted it as final proof of an assertion, such as "all have sinned" (Rom. 3:9ff.). In Romans 10 and 11 there are numerous passages in which Paul used a quotation from the Old Testament as the clinching point, often the only point, in his argument (10:18f.; 11:7f., 26).

In other passages Paul proclaimed that it was indeed God who spoke in the Old Testament, for the gospel was something He "promised beforehand through his prophets in the holy scriptures" (Romans 1:2). Paul went so far as to use the noun, "the Scripture," when he meant God, for example in the sentence, "For the scripture says to Pharoah, 'I have raised you up for the very purpose of showing my power in you'" (Rom. 9:17). We do the same thing today when quoting our authorities. Mothers mean the same thing when they ask, "What does the Baby Book say?" as when they ask, "What does Dr. Spock say?"

Not only did Paul use the Old Testament as if it were his authority. He also made general statements that seem to express that sentiment. He took legal statements of the Old Testament law verbatim, for example, in the quotation, "Cursed be every one who does not abide by all things written in the book of the law, and do them" (Gal. 3:10). Paul's quoting implies acceptance of the truth of this particular statement. But even more, the statement itself is so inclusive it appears to say that Paul accepted the whole Old Testament law as God's standard of acceptance.

Yet he went on to declare that the Jews were entirely mistaken in their appeal to the Old Testament law as the means for salvation. Salvation comes only in Christ, according to Paul, and so he rejects the law as the key to the Old Testament in favor of God's promise as the key to it. In any complex book it is necessary to choose one out of the various possible themes as the key to interpretation. The Old Testament, being a library of books written over one thousand years, requires the choice of an interpretive key far more than most works. The Jews chose the Old Testament commandments as the heart of the matter. Paul chose God's promises.

CHILDHOOD SIMPLIFICATION

The law given in Deuteronomy proclaimed that those who obeyed the law would have life (28:1). Paul said, "That is true, but no one has ever been able to obey the Old Testament law, and so a new way of salvation has been offered in Christ." Apparently, he accepted the Old Testament law as God's demand, the standard which men will have to reach if they wish to earn acceptance before God. God's aim in giving the law, however, was not that men might earn acceptance, but that they might learn humility, might learn that only by His gracious acceptance could they be acceptable to Him. In Paul's mind God is like a tennis coach who took a cocky new member of his team and beat him 6-0 to show him that he still had a lot to learn.

The law was only temporary, like the guardian of a minor child (Gal. 3:23f). The eternal part of the Old Testament is God's promise of free acceptance (Rom. 4), which preceded in time the law given to Moses and stands above the law. The law once had a temporary function that was good. Its object was to lead all men to recognize that they are sinners (Gal. 3: 19) who cannot help themselves (Rom. 7:7-23). The law does not give life, but kills (2 Cor. 3:6), for all it does is condemn men without giving them the power to change their own lives (Rom. 11:32, 7:10). Power comes only in Christ's love.

We often find ourselves in a similar conflict today in trying to decide how to bring up our children. We are torn between an instinct to lay down the law, enforced by punishment, and an impulse to teach by loving and being intimately involved with them. Whether the former method ever works in the long run is debated, but certainly the approach of loving involvement is the only way to enhance the growth and raise the standards of those who are old enough to think and decide for themselves.

REJECTED STANDARD

In addition to his rejection of the law as the way to salvation, Paul also rejected a substantial amount of it as a way of life for those who are Christians and have been given the gift of salvation already. He declared himself indifferent concerning Sabbath observance (Rom. 14:5). Even food offered to idols, which was an abomination to a Jew, was no problem for him. He said that what a man eats has no direct effect on his relationship to God and so everyone should eat whatever he thinks is right (Rom. 14:2f). This is like saying today that whether one smokes and drinks or not has no direct bearing on God's acceptance. Here Paul echoed Jesus' teaching that had become the practice of the Church, at least outside Israel (Gal. 2:12).

Not only did Paul ignore the two central Jewish practices of food and Sabbath observance, he even rejected the heart of the Old Covenant, the demand that all God's people be circumcised (Gen. 17:14). Paul virtually reversed the commandment, saying that any Gentile who became circumcised would be "severed from Christ" (Gal. 5:4). In this radical rejection Paul is like some young people today who burn the American flag rather than salute it because they think that modern America with its militarism, racism, and poverty is the opposite of the ideal America for which the flag once stood. As Paul looked upon continued circumcision as an affirmation of the legalistic Jewish *status quo,* so radicals today look upon the American flag as a symbol of those who support what they see as the unjust American *status quo.*

In fact Paul seems to reject all the detail of the Old Testament law when he says, "He who loves his neighbor has fulfilled the law" (Rom. 13:8). Here is Paul's principle of interpretation: love is God's standard, and only those Old Testament laws which are based on love have any bearing on the life of a Christian. This means, of course, that love, which is the presence of the Holy Spirit (Rom. 5:5), is more important than the law, for it stands above the law, judging it, just as Jesus taught.

For Paul it seems that the Old Testament Law as authority in the Jewish sense is completely rejected. The legal idea that salvation can come by obedience to the law is rejected in favor of God's promise of free acceptance, a promise made to Abraham and fulfilled in Christ. The commandments of the law are rejected because all they did was convince men that they were sinners, a task no longer needed now that men see Christ. The commandments may be of some use for Christian life, but only insofar as they conform to the law of love, which means that the commandments are not really authoritative. Only love is. This is precisely the kind of idea that lies behind modern civil disobedience: "I accept the law's demand as long as it is a just law." This means that the individual's own sense of what is just is his ultimate authority, not the law. This modern theory arose from the New Testament proclamation that the Christian's ultimate authority is the love of God which is at work within him.

THE REST OF THE NEW TESTAMENT

PRESENT POWER

The rest of the New Testament speaks in somewhat stronger tones of the authority of the Old Testament than do Jesus and Paul. For example, we read in one of the later letters that ". . . no prophecy ever came by the impulse of man, but men moved by the Holy Spirit spoke from God" (2 Pet. 1:21). The difficulty in this saying is that the meaning and extent of the word "prophecy" is not clear. It probably does not refer to all prophecy in the Old Testament, because there is false prophecy found there (1 Ki. 22:23). It may refer to all the books of the prophets, or it may refer only to the forecast of future events made in them. Alternatively, this saying may refer to prophets in the early church (1 Cor. 12:10). Certainly it means "true prophets," but the ambiguity over who these are means that this passage cannot be used to prove anything about the Old Testament in general. It is like saying, "All great movies are worth seeing." That may be true, but is not much help on Saturday night over the dinner table when a decision has to be made on what to see.

A more specific statement, seemingly referring to the whole of the Old Testament and not just to prophecy, is found in another late letter: "All scripture is inspired by God and profitable for teaching, for reproof, for correction, and for training in righteousness" (2 Tim. 3:16). The difficulty with this saying is that it could equally well be translated, "Every Scripture inspired by God is also profitable for teaching." If this is the case, then it is not clear how we judge which Scriptures are inspired by God. This lack of a standard then "inspires" readers to read in their own standard unconsciously, but this is not then taking the passage at its (limited) word.

God's speaking through the Old Testament by means of the Holy Spirit is mentioned many times in the New Testament, as when Acts 4:24f. reports a prayer beginning: "Sovereign Lord . . . who by the mouth of our father David, thy servant, didst say by the Holy Spirit," (followed by a quotation from Ps. 2). This same theme is found in the Epistle to the Hebrews, where quotations from the Old Testament are several times prefaced by the phrase, "As the Holy Spirit says," or something similar (3:7, 9:8, 10:15). In the early church the Holy Spirit was understood as God's interpreter, so that referring a statement to the Spirit means it has God's authority, just as the United States' president's press secretary speaks with the authority of the president.

PAST PREROGATIVE

While there are strong statements affirming the authority of the Old Testament in the books we have been discussing, there are also some statements that indicate that in certain respects it is outdated. As in the teaching of Jesus and Paul, once again in the rest of the New Testament there is evidence that the ritual law was not held to be eternally valid for all Christians, as the Jews thought it was for all God's People. Acts 15, the report of the so-called "Jerusalem Council" when Paul and the original Apostles gathered to thresh out the problem of the law, says that Gentile Christians are not required to obey Jewish ritual law. Some participants in the conference thought all Christians should be circumcised, that is, should become Jews before becoming Christians (15:5). But this view was rejected (15:11). Old Testament laws concerning clean and unclean animals, kosher foods, and eating with non-Jews, were almost all rejected as not important for Christians, though some exceptions were given (15:20). The council apparently did not go all the way with Jesus' teaching that nothing that a man eats can harm him spiritually (Mark 7), nor with Paul's contention that eating food offered to idols cannot harm a man (1 Cor. 8). It did, however, accept the principle that the vast majority of the laws which the Jews followed were not of importance for Gentile Christians. Christians believed that their whole life-situation had changed and so their rules for living changed, too. The Jews were soldiers at war, living under strict discipline, but Christians were at peace because Christ had won the war, and so they could live under the freedom of civilians.

This same principle was expounded by the author of the

Epistle to the Hebrews. The whole cultic system of Judaism is rejected by Hebrews on the ground that Christ has fulfilled the sacrificial requirements of God for all time. The Jewish system could not do this and so the "former commandment is set aside because of its weakness and uselessness, (for the law made nothing perfect)" (Heb. 7:18f). The first covenant is called "obsolete and growing old," "ready to vanish away" (8:13). The old sacrifices could not "perfect the conscience of the worshiper" (9:9), "for it is impossible that the blood of bulls and goats should take away sins" (10:4). This, of course, was directly opposed to the sacrificial law of the Old Testament, which said that by the blood of a bull a man's sin could be taken away (Lev. 4:20).

The theory expressed in Hebrews is fairly subtle, for the Old Testament is the "shadow" of which the New Testament is the "reality." The old sacrifices have some value, but Christ's sacrifice alone brings forgiveness. This rejection of the Jewish cult as inadequate is not in keeping with the law as given in Leviticus. On the other hand, it echoes some strains of prophetic thought. Most of the great prophets at one time or another denounced the cultic system, either for its abuses or because it was made a substitute for righteous living (e.g., Amos 5:21ff., Is. 1:11). Thus Hebrews can be said to be adopting one of the strains of thought in the Old Testament in rejecting the cult.

It often happens that man has to choose one or the other strand of his heritage as basic, even though in the past it had been thought that there was no conflict between the two. In the Civil War period a choice had to be made between "all men are created equal" and the constitution's allowance of slavery. The nation chose equality and so had to amend the constitution to forbid slavery. Similarly, the early Church chose the freedom of faith as the heart of the Old Testament message and so rejected the slavery of ritual living.

POSSIBLE CONCLUSIONS

LIFE, NOT RITUAL

All the writers of the New Testament follow Jesus' example in rejecting the religious ritual of the Old Testament. The essential principle upon which He acted was that the external actions of religion cannot be put on the same level as compassion for people. Jesus did not spend His life in churches. He spent it in slums and ghettos where people were in need of Him.

In Israel ritual had become an impediment to doing God's will. As many Christians today think God's chief demand is that we go to church, so Jews of Jesus' time thought that obeying the ritual law was the center of a godly life. The Jews had implicitly stated the issue this way: God is more concerned about religion than He is about the rest of life. Jesus answered this mistaken view of God by saying, forget the ritual; it has no importance in itself, for God is interested in people, in all of life.

A further defect in Old Testament ritual was that it prevented outsiders, Gentiles, from joining God's people. As today our 19th century church music often drives away 20th century people, so the Old Testament ritual law, with its identification with one nation, prevented men of other nations from joining God's people. So the early church discarded the ritual law of the Old Testament and immediately reached the Gentile nations in a way that Jewish preaching never could.

But does rejection of ritual law mean that the moral law of the Old Testament is still binding upon Christians? That is the viewpoint of many today, based principally on Jesus' reference to six of the ten commandments (Mark 10:19). The difficulty with this theory is that Jesus did not lay any great stress on Old Testament commandments. Instead, He said that two things were central: following Him and love of God and all men. Is it not possible that Jesus thus placed Himself on the side of those who say that a true life cannot be lived by memorizing moral rules any more than by obeying ritual law? True life is personal, following Him and loving others. As a marriage relationship that was based on obeying laws would be superficial and phoney, so also our relationship to God and our neighbor can be true and loving only if it flows spontaneously out of what we are inside.

GIFT, NOT LAW

If Paul is a true interpreter of Jesus' thought, it is certain that that was His meaning. Paul proclaimed many times that the law is of no importance to Christians, meaning by this not just the ritual law, but even more importantly the moral law of the Old Testament. He conceded that the law had once been useful, in the childhood of Israel, for it had convinced the people of their sinfulness. But he was adamantly opposed to the Jewish theory that salvation could be earned by obedience to the Old Testament law. As a psychiatrist does not give his patient a book of laws, but helps him to become a new person, so also the salvation offered in Christ is the power for a whole new life.

The Jewish theory was never true, for a loving, personal relationship can never be earned, and is especially untrue since free salvation has been offered in Christ. The law is not even necessary any longer for convincing men of their sin, for looking at Christ does that. The law is certainly of no use in living the Christian life because all it does is lead men into despair and greater sin. All that a Christian needs in order to live the life God intends is the power of love, for love is all that is important in the law. When a man has been living on bread and water for months, he doesn't need a nutrition book to bring him health, he needs solid food. So also men do not need instructions to enable them to love, they need to be loved and so enabled to love.

Does this mean that the whole Old Testament is to be discarded? No, it doesn't, for the Old Testament is not mainly law. The Jews misunderstood the Old Testament when they thought that the Law was its heart. The heart of the Old Testament is in fact God's action in history by which He revealed Himself to be a loving yet chastening Master. History was the center of Israel's faith, for even the Law begins with history: "I am the Lord your God who brought you up out of the land of Egypt." That was God's gift to His people — rescue from slavery. The center of the Old Testament is good news: the Lord is a gracious God who has rescued, and continues to rescue, His people. The question this emphasis on God's action raises is whether all the reports of God's actions in the Old Testament are equally authoritative.

LOVE, NOT HATE

The teaching of Jesus and the New Testament seems to say that these reports are not all equal. The Old Testament has many stories in which atrocities are perpetrated against cities and tribes, supposedly at the instigation of the Lord. Hatred of the outsider is often proclaimed as the reverse side of Israel's self-understanding as God's chosen people. Yet there were many prophets in the Old Testament who spoke against national pride, against hatred of foreigners, against aggressive war. Jesus chose these prophets as His allies, the way a Supreme Court justice selects those precedents which confirm his judgment of the case at hand.

"You can't believe everything you read," seems to have been Jesus' motto, because He denied the idea found in the Old Testament that God ever intends man to fight his neighbor, even if provoked. This denunciation of hatred, coupled with denunciation of ritual, was the outcome of Jesus' own way of life that said, "God cares most of all for common people in their ordinary, daily lives." Much of the report of God's actions in Israel's history stresses His care for His people, sometimes shown in rescue, sometimes shown in punishment. It is this theme of Old Testament history towards which Jesus points us in our search for its continuing authority.

PROMISE, NOT POWER

The trouble with the Old Testament was that it was only a shadow that had to take a subordinate role once the reality had arrived in Christ. We are intrigued by a shadow coming around a corner, but forget it once its owner has caught up with it. Hebrews speaks of the sacrificial system in this way. It was useful in reminding men of their sin, but had no power, for it could not bring forgiveness. Christ is the great sacrifice towards which the system pointed, for which it had been waiting. Once the promise is fulfilled, it is of no more interest.

It was on this same ground that Paul rejected the whole law. He saw God's promise made to Abraham as the great foundation stone of Israel's faith, and so the law which came many years later was only of temporary and subordinate interest. Once the promise reached fruition in Christ, even the law's temporary value ceased. It had no power of itself. It simply pointed forward to Him who did have power.

In a similar vein the Constitution of the United States embodies a great promise in its statement, "All men are created equal." This promise was kept from black Americans by the law for years, first by slavery, then by "separate but equal" laws which were inherently unequal. The promise finally came to legal fulfillment in 1954 when the Supreme Court tore down segregation. But even that decision is still mainly promise, for the reality of equality has not come to fulfillment. Once black Americans reach the promised land of equality, the old laws and decisions which promised equality will become only historical relics, interesting for historians but of no practical importance.

Not even Israel's history, which knew many promises and fulfillments, could ultimately be seen as anything but the greatest of promises. Israel never reached the peace and fellowship with God towards which she was heading. She made advances through God's love, but stepped back through her own willfulness. After the highpoint had been reached in David's reign, the people ever after looked forward in steadfast, assured hope to another David, a greater David, who would come and bring the world-wide peace and true love of God and man for which they longed.

Finally, He came. He was the end of the Old Testament and the standard by which it must be judged. Its ritual law is bypassed because Christ was interested in life, not ritual. Its legal system is turned aside because life comes by God's gift, not by law. Its history is seen as one in which God gives to His people, but wherever there is hatred of others, it is rejected because God is love. The whole of the Old Testament, but mainly its recitation of God's acts in history, points forward to Christ. Insofar as it points to Christ, it is authoritative, for that reason. The truth is that the Old Testament has lost the authority by which it once stood by itself on its own feet. Now it stands as a signpost whose object is not to call attention to itself, but to point the traveler on his way to the One who is the Authority.

2

New Testament Claims to Authority

If the Old Testament is not an absolute standard in itself, does this mean that the New Testament writers simply put themselves in the place of the Old Testament? No, it does not. The New Testament writers were of two minds concerning the Old Testament, accepting its authority, but rejecting some central themes in it. Oddly enough, they saw themselves in the same light. They claimed that they were the true witnesses and interpreters of God's act in Christ, but also admitted that their jurisdiction was not unrestricted. They were like our Supreme Court justices who sometimes appear to have final authority, though they know that they stand under the Constitution. Absolute power to command allegiance — intellectual, emotional, and active — belongs only to the living Christ, who is God's presence in the Church today, as He was among the disciples during His lifetime.

This means that the teaching of Jesus is the source of the standing of the New Testament as the unique constitutional document of the Church. Since it has this great importance, His understanding must be investigated. The Gospel of John will be considered apart from the other three Gospels, because it presents a somewhat different emphasis than the others. The claims of Paul will be discussed thirdly, followed, finally, by the witness of the Acts of the Apostles. In each case it needs to be asked how the author understands himself: like a military officer who simply commands; like an expert who presents his credentials to convince others of his authority; or like a consultant who merely advises and hopes the advice is convincing.

JESUS

Prophetic Voice

It was characteristic of Jesus' experience that when He taught, people "were astonished at his teaching, for he taught them as one who had authority, and not as the scribes" (Mark 1:22). Scribes taught by continual reference to the Old Testament and to the discussions of rabbis and scribes who had lived before them. They saw their job as handing down and interpreting the authoritative tradition which they had been taught, as a master craftsman today hands on his knowledge to an apprentice. Jesus, on the other hand, did not see Himself in that role. Instead of handing down tradition, He created it. He proclaimed the will of God and the news of the coming of God's Kingdom simply on His own authority. This amazed the people, because a prophet speaking on the basis of His own consciousness of God's will had not been heard in Israel for centuries — the one possible exception being John the Baptist.

Sometimes Jesus not only spoke apart from tradition but, in fact, rejected tradition. The Old Testament allowed and even demanded retaliation, but Jesus said, "But I say to you, Do not resist one who is evil" (Matt. 5:39). Six times the phrase, "But I say to you," is repeated in this chapter of Matthew, each time overruling past tradition as the Supreme Court did in its 1954 School Desegregation ruling. In speaking this way, Jesus presented Himself as the One His listeners should obey. Sometimes He gave reasons for His commands (Matt. 5:34, 45), but more often He simply spoke unequivocably of what He knew to be right. He was like a father answering a child's "why?" with, "That's the way things are."

Not only did He know His words took precedence over the Law of Moses, but He also declared that they had wider application, for His words are for all the world: "Go therefore and make disciples of all nations . . . teaching them to observe all that I have commanded you" (Matt. 28:19f.). Unlike the law of Moses which many Jews thought was only for Israel, the teaching of Jesus is for all men. And for all time: "Heaven and earth will pass away, but my words will not pass away" (Mark 13:31). That may perhaps be a hyperbolic statement, a typical example of oriental exaggeration, but the substance of the saying is remarkable, for Jesus claimed that His words have more reality, and are nearer to God's intentions for man, than even the physical universe.

The Way to Life

Because His words have this ultimate importance, following them is vital for men. Jesus said that every one who hears and obeys His words is like "a wise man who built his house upon the rock" so that not even a hurricane or an earthquake could demolish it (Matt. 7:24f.). Those who do not obey Him are like men who build houses on earth-fill, or in slide areas: they have no chance of surviving the onslaughts that life will bring. Indeed it is not only the storms of life that are a concern in Jesus' words, but also the question of eternity.

The true and lasting life, which the Jew sought in the law, can come only to those who are willing to abandon every security and follow Jesus (Mark 10:21). As sacrifice is essential for success in sports, so also it is required at the depths of life. Eternal life, acceptance by God into His kingdom, comes only to those who will give their lives to Him, "For whoever would save his life will lose it; and whoever loses his life for my sake . . . will save it" (Mark 8:35). The word "life" as Jesus used it had two different senses. The life we are called to lose is this present life, the worldly standards of success and power, and for some even physical life itself. The life that will be gained is found in relationship with other people, God's favor, eternal life. This kind of absolute commitment, laying life on the line, is rare in the modern world. It is found mainly among revolutionaries, both Christian and Communist, in under-developed parts of the world. The Albert Schweitzers of the mid-twentieth century are rare, but not extinct.

The crucial question is a man's attitude toward Jesus, at least that was what He claimed: "For whoever is ashamed of me and of my words in this adulterous and sinful generation, of him will the Son of Man also be ashamed" (Mark 8:38). But, " . . . every one who acknowledges me before men, I also will acknowledge before my Father" (Matt. 10:32). Thus it seems clear that it is not simply acceptance of Jesus' words as authoritative that He called for, but for the commitment of life to Him which may involve giving up everything. Unlike Communism, which calls a man to an abstract ideal, a classless society, Christ calls a man to personal involvement with Himself.

It is His claim to be the "Son of Man" that summarizes much of Jesus' authority. The Son of Man is to be the Judge on the Final Day (Matt. 25:31), and the standard that He will use is the way men have treated Him. He identifies Himself with all of needy mankind, so loving Him means reaching out to all those in need, for "as you did it to one of the least of these my brethren, you did it to me" (Matt. 25:40). The "Judge" is just the opposite of an American judge who will disqualify himself if he has any personal relationship to the defendent. The Son of Man is like the justices in small towns in Mexico who know all the people in the town, are related to most of them, and judge personally rather than impartially.

Personal Standing

The basis of Jesus' claim to authority seems to be His relationship to God. He spoke of God in an intimate way as His Father, drawing His disciples into this same relationship when He taught them the Lord's Prayer. The beginning of that prayer is the word "Abba," a diminuitive that is best explained by our word, "Daddy." The Jews had always thought of God as the Father of Israel, but they had not spoken of Him in this intimate way. Intimacy implies familiarity, a close relationship that Jesus clearly experienced with God. He continually spoke of God as "My Father" (Matt. 10:32), implying that He stood in a special relationship to Him. The most explicit expression of this relationship is given by Jesus in these words: "All things have been delivered to me by my Father; and no one knows the Son except the Father, and no one knows the Father except the Son and anyone to whom the Son chooses to reveal him" (Matt. 11:27). Here Jesus speaks like one of Howard Hughes' assistants. Hughes is almost never seen by the public, so when his views are sought, they always must come through his assistants who alone know him and his wishes and can make them public.

Here Jesus claims to speak for God, to be His press agent, the only One able and authorized to make Him known. The audacity of this claim has been the basis for its rejection by many people, for they say that God is known by many means. Many men have been prophets pointing to Him. Jesus did not deny that, however, for He knew of the Old Testament prophets and did not deny the validity of their proclamation. What seems to be at stake here is the distinction between "knowing" someone and "knowing about" them. There are famous men I know about, but I do not know them because I have not met them. Many people have "known about" God and proclaimed what they knew, but this objective, intellectual knowledge is not what men basically need. What they need is personal knowledge of God, a relationship to Him, and this "knowing God" is what Jesus claimed to offer. Jesus is the living presence of God, the One to Whom men can respond.

The question He posed for His hearers, which the Church has posed for the world ever since, is simply whether men will accept or reject Him. Those who accept Him come to know God through Him, but if we reject Him He says we have rejected God: "He who rejects me rejects him who sent me" (Luke 10:16). Jesus is like the "advance man" in a political campaign who goes into each new city before the candidate and makes all the decisions and draws up all the plans for the campaign. If any one wishes to serve or be served by the candidate, he must do so by knowing and working with and for the advance man. So Jesus is God's advance man, knowing His will, making His decisions, accepting or rejecting in His name.

The Ultimate Choice

It is clear that Jesus claimed the allegiance of all men, for He said their eternal well-being depended on their attitude and action with regard to Himself and His teaching. But why should we accept His authority? Why did the people who heard Him accept it? Probably because of the impression He made upon them. He offered no convincing proof of His claims, for the healings He performed were seen by His enemies who rejected Him, as well as by His friends who followed Him. He based His teaching to a certain degree on the Old Testament, but most of what He taught was not so based, and sometimes even opposed the Old Testament. Apparently, He was an imposing figure. It was the kind of man He was that convinced people that His word was true. He did not often give arguments to support His assertions, though occasionally He did. He sometimes appealed to common sense (Mark 7:18), at other times to the character of God (Matt. 5:45), but mostly He appealed to no authority beyond Himself. He simply claimed to speak for God.

There have been many such charismatic figures in history, men who were followed simply because of the strength of their character, or convictions, or eloquence. During the past generation the world saw three such men in Adolf Hitler, Winston Churchill and Franklin Roosevelt. They each came to power at a time of great national weakness and despair, brought to their positions because they convinced people they could stem the tide. None of them could prove at the beginning how great their influence and achievements would be, but they convinced others to take a chance on them because the alternatives (Communism, Chamberlain and Hoover) were more frightening.

Jesus, however, was able to convince people to follow Him even though the alternative was not demonstrably a failure. The Jewish Law had held the nation together for centuries and had continued to exercise its power even under the Romans. Jesus' personal involvement with those whom He met, however, was enough to convince them that He was right and the scribes and the legal system were wrong. There is no reason that can be given to demonstrate which is the right choice. It is a matter of faith, of commitment, of decision, the most central of human actions. Accepting or rejecting the call of God that comes to men in Jesus is the ultimate choice, for by it man's whole life is determined. That is the basis of Jesus' authority — that He appeared to men as the call of God to them.

THE GOSPEL OF JOHN

Transparent Pressure

In the Gospel of John there are clear statements made on issues that the Synoptics (the first three Gospels) bring up only ambiguously, for example, the meaning of calling God, "Father." The Synoptics report Jesus' referring to God as "My Father," but do not make an issue of it, for the disciples are also to call Him, "Our Father." In John, however, there is unequivocal meaning given to this relationship between Jesus and God: He ". . . called God his Father, making himself equal with God" (5:18). Whether or not that was what Jesus meant by the title, it is certainly an idea that is pressed home by this Gospel.

The same charge is brought against Him, of making Him-

self equal to God, when He says, "I and the Father are one"
(10:30), and the charge is not completely off base, for later He
says, "He who has seen me has seen the Father" (14:9). In
support of these claims we read several times that Jesus said
that the Son of Man descended from heaven (3:13), or that
"God sent the Son into the world" (3:17), or "I have come
down from heaven" (6:38). The image that this presents is of
the heir to the throne being sent out from London to travel
around the empire, speaking as the stand-in for his father the
king.

All of these claims are elaborations of the initial proclamation of the gospel: "In the beginning was the Word, and the
Word was with God, and the Word was God . . . all things
were made through him . . . and the Word became flesh and
dwelt among us" (1:1, 3, 14). This is the understanding the
author of the Gospel of John had of the person of Jesus. He
described Him as the Mind of God (for that is what "Word"
basically means here). When he said, "The Word became
flesh," he meant that when we listen to Jesus, we are listening
to God Himself speaking, for Jesus' words are the authoritative
words of God: "My teaching is not mine but his who sent me"
(7:16).

In the Synoptic Gospels, it is implied that Jesus speaks
God's words, but almost always it is Jesus' own personal authority that is stressed in the Synoptics, rather than His relationship to God. The reader knows that the relationship stands behind His words, but in the Synoptics Jesus seldom made this
point explicit. This means that Jesus Himself, as He appeared
to His listeners, was authority enough without a constant reference being made to God. In this sense the Synoptics, perhaps, could be said to proclaim the authority of Jesus even more
than does the Gospel of John, even though the latter goes out
of its way to proclaim that Jesus is God's Word. The difference
is between a man who stands and speaks his mind on the assumption that what he says and how he says it will be convinc-

ing (Synoptics), and another who presents his credentials and references before speaking in order to prejudice his listeners in his favor (John).

Demonstrable Power

The Gospel of John also emphasizes the importance of the healings Jesus performed as the basis for belief, as the evidence of His standing. The subscript of the original version of the book makes this point: "These (signs) are written that you may believe that Jesus is the Christ, the Son of God, and that believing you may have life in his name" (20:31). The "signs" are not only healings, though these are mentioned often (11:47f.); everything He did was a sign, a pointer to His meaning. For example, the cleansing of the Temple was a sign of His reforming zeal. More important still, His resurrection was the sign of God's approval of Him, just as the reappearance of a forgotten official on a Communist platform is a sign of the Party's approval of him.

The chief signs, or works, are the healings, however, and of these, John reports Jesus as saying, "The works which the Father has granted me to accomplish, these very works which I am doing, bear me witness that the Father has sent me" (5:36). They do not "prove" His authority, for the rulers are able to reject them (11:47f.), but they do "bear witness" for those who are willing to see. The stress in this Gospel is on those who believe because they see.

The clearest example of this tendency to stress "seeing is believing" is given in the words attributed to Jesus: "Even though you do not believe me, believe the works" (John 10:38). The implication of this saying seems to be that the "works" speak for themselves, and so should convince an observer of their divine origin. Men constantly point to their works as signs of the higher authority they obey. The President of the United States, when challenged on his dedication to

Civil Rights, urged that he not be judged on campaign rhetoric but by the achievements of his administration.

The Gospel of John thus presents evidence to back up the authority of Jesus' words. It points to His works, and also claims that Jesus could speak as He did because He is the Word of God. The Synoptics, on the other hand, simply show that Jesus spoke with authority, so that many people were willing to follow Him. It is fairly clear, once we think about it, which of these two approaches is more forceful and appealing, for we are moved by those who confront us and touch us, much more than by those who argue that we ought to be moved.

Conclusion: Proof or Appeal?

The decision to which Christ calls man is an absolute, moral decision, a commitment concerning the direction and meaning of life. If reasons are given to us why we *ought* to decide one way, we can think up many reasons to oppose them. When, however, we are simply confronted by One who says, "Follow Me," we realize that we are not confronted by an intellectual problem with reasons for and against, but by a Person who demands an absolutely personal decision from us.

The Gospel of John, in presenting reasons for Jesus' call, allows that call to be debated. The Synoptics leave no room for debate, for they bring us face to face with One who demands a "Yes" or a "No," and our whole life hangs on our answer. It is the kind of decision a girl faces when a man says, "I love you." There is no room for debate, only for response. Either she accepts his love and responds in kind, or she rejects it.

PAUL

Paul's letters are very different from the Gospels, for he does not speak at any length about the authority of Jesus' preaching. Instead of the preaching *of* Jesus, preaching *about* Jesus dominates his epistles. The substance of Paul's teaching

concerned the *meaning* of, rather than simply the *facts* of,
Jesus' life, death, and resurrection. The crucial questions that
must be raised with respect to Paul are these: what made him
develop his theology as he did? On whose authority did he base
his teaching? In discussing this we will not try to delve into the
background of his teaching, seeing where it agrees with Jesus
and the Apostles, but will concentrate on Paul's own claims to
authority, where he himself believed his authority to lie.

Second Hand Reporters

He certainly looked upon Jesus as *the* authority and referred
to His teaching on occasion as the foundation for his own remarks: "To the married I give charge, not I but the Lord, that
the wife should not separate from her husband" (1 Cor. 7:10).
Here Paul, apparently, is referring to Jesus' teaching on divorce
which is recorded in all the Synoptics. It seems that Paul had
received a certain number of the sayings of Jesus, but this is the
only time he explicitly leans upon Jesus' authority. There are
many other times when his teaching could have been supported
by the teaching of Jesus, and perhaps was dependent upon it,
but he does not elsewhere make the connection. The likelihood is that Paul knew more of Jesus' sayings than he used,
and so the fact that he rarely mentions them means that he did
not think his authority basically lay in the tradition handed
down from Jesus. In this respect, Paul was like an experienced
cook who refers at times to a recipe book, but far more often
goes her own way, using recipes that come from personal experience.

Elsewhere in this same letter, 1 Corinthians, Paul refers to
the tradition of the gospel that he received, but does not mention from whom it came: "For I delivered to you as of first importance what I also received, that Christ died for our sins . . .
that he was buried, that he was raised . . . and that he appeared" (1 Cor. 15:3-5). This is basically the account that was
preached by the first apostles, according to Acts. The appear-

ances to Peter, to the five hundred, to James, and to all the apostles (vv. 5-7), were initially reported by those involved. The accounts were collected and many preachers referred to them. Probably, Paul received this information when he first became a Christian.

Paul uses here two technical words for the handing down of religious tradition, "receive" and "deliver." This indicates that Paul saw himself in a chain which linked the disciples, who had witnessed the life, death, and resurrection of Jesus, to those who later believed. Here it seems that Paul sees himself as having a derived authority, an authority that is dependent upon his proper standing with the Church as a whole, and especially his accurate handing down of the tradition he had received. He was like the member of a fraternity or order that has unwritten rituals. The members learn the rituals and hand them down from generation to generation, authority lying in the fact of having "received" and "handed on" the tradition, not in any originality or creativity.

Primary Witness

But wait a minute! The last line of Paul's account of the primitive preaching is this: "Last of all, as to one untimely born, he appeared also to me" (1 Cor. 15:8). Paul has duly set himself in the line of apostolic tradition, but then, at the end he claims to be one of the sources of that tradition. The heart of the gospel of the early church lay in its witness to the resurrection of Jesus, and the leaders in the early church were those who had been witnesses to His appearances. They had been singled out by the appearance of Christ to them as men who would be the foundation of the Church, and so Paul's claim to be a witness to the resurrection meant that he, too, was claiming to be one of the foundation stones of the church. In essence he is saying to the rest of the Church: "I have equal authority with the apostles who knew Jesus in the flesh, because I am also a witness to His resurrection." This claim to equality must have seemed to the other apostles somewhat impudent, like the demands of DeGaulle at the end of the Second World War that he be given an equal place in the Big Four, even though France was down and out and DeGaulle had not even been elected to represent her.

Paul's claim to equal standing lay therefore *ultimately* in Christ, but *immediately* in his conversion experience. He rejected the idea that he was simply a recipient of tradition who was passing it on. He rejected the contention of the original apostles that he ought to submit to them because he had not known Jesus in the flesh. He claimed to have the word of Christ Himself behind his preaching: "For I would have you know, brethren, that the gospel which was preached by me is not man's gospel. For I did not receive it from man, nor was I taught it, but it came through a revelation of Jesus Christ. For you have heard of my former life in Judaism, how I persecuted the church . . . (but God) was pleased to reveal his Son to me, in order that I might preach him among the Gentiles" (Gal. 1:11-16). All of Paul's preaching, the whole development of his theology, is based upon this one experience.

Paul was absolutely convinced that he had seen the risen Christ and concluded from that that Jesus had indeed been acting for God instead of against Him. All Paul's theology comes from that one basic conclusion. Such absolute convictions are not uncommon, not only in the field of religion, but in all fields. The basis for all great movements is a conviction like Paul's. Marx saw the oppression of workers by capitalists and was overcome by the belief that this evil and all evil would end if private property were done away with. The American Revolution took place because a small group of men strongly believed that the colonies had an inherent right to be free. Paul's experience was like that in its effect on him, for there was no possibility of arguing with him over it. When he preached the message of God's acts in Christ, he believed that his preaching had divine authority, was in fact "the word of God" (1 Thess. 2:13).

Uncertain Trumpet

On the question of the Christian way of life, however, Paul was somewhat ambiguous in different letters. Sometimes he claimed absolute authority: "I am bold enough in Christ to command you to do what is required" (Philem. 8); "Now we command you, brethren, in the name of our Lord Jesus Christ" (2 Thess. 3:6). On some issues it seems that Paul believed that his knowledge of the gospel entitled him to speak in Christ's name.

At other times Paul did not claim the authority of Christ for what he said. At the beginning of this discussion of Paul we referred to his saying, "I give charge, (actually) not I but the Lord." In other parts of that same letter he shows an important distinction between Christ's teaching and his own. Two verses on, he said: "To the rest I say, not the Lord" (1 Cor. 7:12). Apparently, Paul had looked through his list of Jesus' sayings and found nothing to cover the subject, so he told what he thought. Further on in the same chapter he made this explicit when he said, "Now concerning the unmarried, I have no command of the Lord, but I give my opinion as one who by the Lord's mercy is trustworthy" (1 Cor. 7:25). Here Paul is like a husband who answers a question for his absent wife by saying, "I haven't heard her say anything specifically on that subject, but I think I know her well enough to say . . . ."

It seems that Paul would have liked at times to have an authoritative word from Jesus to speak, but he did not, and so he gave his own opinion, and recommended it to his readers, but did not command them. This was his implication at the end of that chapter also, "And in my judgment she is happier if she remains as she is (a widow). And I think that I have the Spirit of God" (1 Cor. 7:40). The gift of the Spirit was not peculiar to apostles, so Paul is simply saying, "My Christian conscience tells me," and not "My apostolic authority commands."

The question this raises for us is, when is Paul speaking only on the basis of his Christian conscience, which we all have and which can reasonably be expected to differ from his on occasion, especially when it concerns our "happiness," and when is he speaking with apostolic authority? Did he think his words were authoritative unless he said otherwise? Or was it only his own opinion unless he said otherwise? This was the same problem the Roman Catholic Church created for itself when it said in 1870 that the Pope is infallible. The Church hedged this claim in, however, by saying that this is only true when he speaks *ex cathedra,* that is, when he says he is infallible.

Conclusion: Authority or Witness

Paul certainly was one of the dominant figures in the early Church, but does he still have authority over the Church today? If we believe that Christ did appear to him on the Damascus road, would this mean that we would look up to him as an authority on the meaning of Christ's life and death? Or would it mean that we would look up to him solely as a witness to the *fact* of the resurrection of Christ, but would take his theology, his deductions from that fact, as his personal opinion? Trying to separate one from the other would have been like listening to Einstein speak about the moral implications of scientific discoveries. We know he was a genius in science, but we don't really know how much that entitled him to speak authoritatively of morality. Paul was certainly a witness to the fact of the resurrection of Jesus. The problem is in deciding how much his deductions from that fact were his own opinion, his preaching to men of his own time, and how much they are the "word of the Lord."

Our problem in following Paul is that he himself admits that his word is not as important as the word of Christ. Yet at times, his word *is* the word of Christ.

LUKE — ACTS

The first section of this chapter, dealing with the Synoptic Gospels, is as close as we can get to the thought of Jesus Himself. The second section, from the Gospel of John, purports to be the words of Jesus but probably as they were filtered through the later understanding of the Church. It is possible that the man who wrote, or at least provided the basic thinking of the Gospel was a close friend of Jesus, one who knew Him well. The third section, on Paul, deals with one who did not know Jesus during His lifetime, but claimed personal authority on the basis of seeing Him after the resurrection. This fourth section deals with a man who neither knew Jesus during His lifetime, nor was a witness to His resurrection. He is a reporter at second hand. In some ways he was a journalist reporting the events as they were delivered to him. In other ways he was an historian shaping the account and the incidents he included to make a coherent and persuasive treatise.

Gospel Interpreter

Luke's own description of how he worked, and what he was trying to do, is found in the Prologue to his Gospel: "Inasmuch as many have undertaken to compile a narrative of the things which have been accomplished among us, just as they were delivered to us by those who from the beginning were eyewitnesses and ministers of the word, it seemed good to me also, having followed all things closely for some time past, to write an orderly account for you, most excellent Theophilus, that you may know the truth concerning the things of which you have been informed" (Luke 1:1-4). In this statement Luke makes no claim to special, personal authority such as we find in Paul and Jesus. Luke claims his reader's acceptance on the grounds that he has done his homework, has listened closely to the witnesses, has compiled all the information he can, and has then put it together into a coherent account.

He claims that his account is "the truth," but the only guarantee he gives of this truth is his own diligence, intelligence, and breadth of acquaintance. He makes no claims to revelations, or to inspiration by the Holy Spirit or to miracles as a guarantee. If Theophilus is a real person (the name means "lover of God" and may simply be a pseudonym for "my Christian reader"), then it is likely that he knew Luke, and so Luke's character was the basis for his authority in this matter. Theophilus knew he could trust Luke, and on that basis Luke sent him this work. On the same basis we write letters to our friends, expecting them to take our word as the truth as far as we know it.

Our problem is that we don't know Luke. We don't know exactly what his standards of truth were. We don't know how closely connected he was with the "eyewitnesses" who are his source. We don't know to what extent his desire to write an "orderly account" caused him to modify the raw materials as they came to him. We do know something about Luke's methods, we think, for most scholars believe that the Gospel of Mark was one of the sources Luke used in writing his Gospel. If that is true (and the subject will be discussed in a later chapter), then we *can* see to a certain extent how closely Luke followed his source in this case. The Gospel is thus like a modern book in which the footnotes can be checked for accuracy.

If Mark was his authority, we can say that in general Luke followed him fairly closely, eliminating details now and then, preferring another account he had received on occasion, but in essence being faithful to Mark's account. We can see specific ways in which Luke modified Mark and so can discount them when we are trying to get to the original material, but by and large he is faithful to the raw material he received. In effect his methods are not far removed from those of a modern biographer who eliminates unnecessary details, rewrites stories, and changes the viewpoint of the work somewhat to express what the biographer understands as the true nature of his subject.

Apostolic Witness

If this is the way Luke wrote his Gospel, must we then deduce that he operated the same way in the Acts of the Apostles? It is reasonable to assume that he did, for Acts is the second volume of the "narrative" he referred to in the Prologue. Probably we can accept him as a reliable witness with regard to the materials that he received, but the problem is that we do not know how much material he had received. A number of passages in Acts have been suggested as quotations, but no original sources have been found, so no check of the accuracy of Luke's quotations in Acts can be made. We cannot have the same certainty about the accuracy of the handing down of tradition in Acts, therefore, as we can in the Gospel of Luke. Nevertheless, there are many details of background in Acts which indicate that Luke had accurate information about the world of the apostles. This implies that his information about the actions of the apostles is liable to have the same kind of veracity. That is as far as we can go in judging the historical authority of Acts. The same problem arises in every historical source that stands by itself. Is Caesar's *Gallic Wars* an accurate portrayal of the events described? Did Thucydides have firsthand information for all of *The Peloponnesian Wars?* Is I Samuel a true account of David's reign? In no case can historical certainty be obtained.

Interpreter

Does the authority of Acts over our life and faith depend to any great degree on its historical certainty? Is it not possible that Luke presents the true meaning of Jesus' death and resurrection even if most of the details of Acts are lengendary rather than historical? As Jesus' parables were fiction that told the truth about life, so it is possible that Acts could fall into the same category. It is certainly not strictly fiction, or even an historical novel; in fact it is becoming clearer as time goes on that Luke was a very good historian whose sources were of great historical value. Nevertheless the question of its accuracy in historical details is secondary to the question of its accuracy in understanding Jesus. Often a portrait, which does not have the detailed accuracy of a photograph, will still be a better representation of its subject, for it can include more of his character than a photograph can.

Acts depends on the authority of the apostles, for Luke is handing down their witness to Christ. Insofar as he conveys the essential message of Jesus' meaning, he is a witness, just as the apostles were. The primary locus of the apostles' authority lay in exactly the same place that it lay with Paul — the fact that they were witnesses to the resurrection of Christ. The central assertion of Peter's first sermon in Acts is this line: "This Jesus God raised up, and of that we all are witnesses" (2:32; cf. 3:15, 5:32, 10:41 also). This one-point message upon which everything stood was like the news that spread through the Allied armies in May of 1945 giving fulfillment to all their hopes: "The War is Over."

By making the resurrection message central, Luke shows that Acts is basically true to the early Church's understanding of herself. All the New Testament books are based on the resurrection of Christ, and so Acts is another authoritative witness to the early Church's essential message. The central point of Acts is not the accurate representation of the details of the apostles' actions and sermons. Rather the central point is the proclamation that God has brought new life for all men in Jesus Christ. In a similar way, the novel *Ben-Hur* was not written to give historical details of the time of Jesus, but to show the effect of Jesus on mankind — then and now. As in Luke-Acts, there are many accurate historical details, but the authority lies elsewhere. The authority of Luke-Acts is not dependent on the historian's assessment of them, but on the message they proclaim.

CONCLUSION

Those early apostolic witnesses are no longer able to speak, but they left a message that the truth about Jesus is to be found in two interdependent ways: the first is through the Spirit, the Spirit of Christ and of God, who is the same now as then; the second is in the writings that these early reporters left for us. The Spirit is first because we only accept the writings as true when we have been convinced by the Spirit. This is not a scientific explanation of "how" we come to believe, but an expression of faith that those who do believe have experienced the presence of God as the decisive factor in their faith. They read the words of Jesus and for some inexplicable reason they say "this must be true." This kind of immediate conviction is like the inspiration of a scientist who suddenly "sees" the theory that will draw together all the facts he has accumulated.

For some people, the only authority lies in the words of Jesus, so that the importance of the New Testament depends upon the accuracy with which it reports His words. But such a theory, that only Jesus' words matter, disagrees with what the Church has always said is its essential message, that Jesus has been raised. Some would see the resurrection as simply confirmation of Jesus' commission by God, the backing His words needed to convince the skeptical. But if Jesus' presence did not impress them, then certainly secondhand stories about empty tombs and ghostly appearances could not fill the gap. If the leader of a nation cannot draw his people together by his presence and words over radio and television, then commentators extolling his feats will certainly fail also.

The resurrection was not simply confirmation of what the disciples knew. It added a whole new dimension to the meaning of Jesus. His death appeared to be condemnation by God, but His resurrection showed that it was the world which was judged instead. His death seemed to signal the end of hope, but His resurrection was a sign of the end of the world, of the victory over death that God was bringing for all. All this was not known during Jesus' lifetime, for then the disciples did not understand anything about Jesus' death and resurrection. Only the resurrection finally declared what God had been doing in Jesus, and so this witness to the resurrection is equally as important as Jesus' own words.

Our western civilization is a word-oriented, intellectual civilization, so we expect God just to speak. We find it difficult to accept the fact that God revealed Himself in a civilization that was action-oriented, so that He was known primarily by what He did. We need this reality of the primary importance of action brought home to us, because far too often we imagine that when we deplore the evils of our society we have done something about them. We talk, and talk is often cheap. God acts, and calls us to follow Him.

The act of God in the resurrection spoke somewhat ambiguously, for a variety of conclusions could be, and were, drawn from it. Paul's conclusions, given in his theology, were those that have had the most effect upon the Church, but as was shown above, he knew the distinction between his own opinion and "the word of Christ." How he distinguished between the two is not clear in most of his letters. What is clear is that Paul, along with the other New Testament writers, believed that Christ (or "the Spirit of Christ") was the supreme authority, and their own writings were a vastly important, but still secondary, authority.

This kind of basic written authority coupled with and subservient to a final living authority is best exemplified in the modern world by the government of Great Britain. Unlike the United States of America, that nation has no written constitution to which all must adhere. What is written is the tradition of English Common Law, made up of thousands of decisions from the past which are "the way things are done," according to the English. Supreme authority, however, resides

in Parliament, which can pass an act to legalize or forbid anything it pleases. So for Christians, according to the New
Testament writers themselves, the New Testament is the
foundation document, but the living Christ is the only One
whom they must follow completely.

3

The Church's Ancient Library

The books of the Bible can be changed anytime the Church decides to change them. Most Christians may not realize it, but the Church is not required to keep just the books it has now. It could decide to alter the selection, either by addition or subtraction. The Bible is the Church's library, and adding or eliminating books is a continual process in most libraries.

This question of which books belong in the Bible is going to become an ever more pressing problem as the spirit of unity between the churches grows. The Roman Catholic Bible is considerably larger than the Protestant Bible, and the Orthodox Churches hold a mediating position between Catholic and Protestant. This is an issue that all must discuss if there is ever to be a genuine unity among them. The object of this chapter is to discuss the origin of the canon (the list of books) of the Bible, and then to see whether we today should accept the decisions of the past.

But do we today need a set of ancient books to guide us? Times have changed so much that any books written two thousand or more years ago could well be completely out of date. In some respects, in particular scientifically, they are out of date. But they may still be normative for us if they supply something that nothing since ancient times could supply. For example, the United States Constitution is an old document, but it provides a basis for the union of all the states, something that would be difficult to find in a modern document. But even if a canon is needed, is the one we have the right one? Are there not a number of books in the Bible that we would be well rid of, and a number of others not in the Bible that it would be well to add?

These are open questions that the Church must decide anew in every generation. Protestant churches have continually affirmed their commitment to the Bible as presently constituted, but whenever they decide to change they can do so. If we do not think about what books belong in the Bible, we are simply accepting the tradition handed down from generations past and not using our minds to the glory of God. Most Christians when asked why they accept this canon answer the way an Appalachian mountaineer once did. When asked why his family always poured the first glass of a bottle of whiskey out on the yard, he answered, "I don't know. We've always done it."

THE OLD TESTAMENT

HOW DID WE GET HERE?

The history of the Old Testament canon is a long and detailed story about which there is still a good deal of ignorance, even among scholars. The general outline is fairly clear, however. The first part of the Old Testament to be accepted as canonical was "The Law," comprised of the first five books, Genesis to Deuteronomy. This group was completed about 500 BC and was accepted by the Jews as supreme authority about 400 BC. "The Law" was the basic authority of Judaism, analogous to the original United States Constitution.

The second section of the canon was called, "The Prophets," and is made up of all the history books from Joshua to Second Kings (known as "the Earlier Prophets") plus all the books containing prophetic utterances, from Isaiah to Zechariah, but excluding Daniel (a group known as "The Later Prophets"). Certainly not later than 200 BC, this group of books was accepted by the Jews as authoritative also, though not quite on the same high level as "The Law." In a certain sense, "The Prophets" are like the Bill of Rights added to the United States Constitution — later additions that clarify but do not supersede the original.

The third section of the Hebrew Canon is called, "The Writings," and included everything else in our present Old Testament (Chronicles, Ezra, Nehemiah, Esther, Job, Psalms, Proverbs, Ecclesiastes, Song of Songs, Lamentations, Daniel). It is not clear when this group first came to be accepted as canonical. It is generally agreed, however, that in AD 90 a Jewish Council was held at Jamnia and settled on these books, the books of our Old Testament, as the official canon of Judaism.

Throughout the first century AD, and even later, there were disputes among the Jews whether certain books should be included. The disputed books were Esther, Proverbs, Ecclesiastes, The Song of Songs, and Ezekiel, all of them but the last being among the Writings. Eventually they were all included, and the Hebrew canon ended up exactly the same as our present Protestant Old Testament. "The Writings" are like the later Amendments to the United States Constitution, debated additions that finally were made authoritative.

Rejected Amendments

The writers of the New Testament used the Old Testament as Scripture, and within the New Testament there are quotations or reminiscences of all the Old Testament books except Obadiah, Nahum, Zephaniah, Esther, Ecclesiastes, Songs of Songs, Ruth, Lamentations, Ezra, Nehemiah, and Chronicles. There are also quotations or reminiscences of a number of other Jewish books, some from the Apocrypha (the extra books of the Greek Old Testament) and some from Jewish writings that no one ever considered to be canonical.

The early Church (after the Age of the Apostles) used the Greek Bible for the most part, since most of the early Christian churches were situated outside of Israel and did not know Hebrew. It is therefore not surprising that their Old Testament contained the extra books that are found in the Greek Bible. The popular understanding of the Old Testament from the second century onward was that it included the Apocrypha as well as the books we have today. A certain number of scholars in the early Church, those who had been instructed in Hebrew, or by Jewish teachers, knew that the Hebrew Bible did not include the extra books, and so these Fathers claimed that the Old Testament should be basically only the Hebrew canon.

The final decision was made about the fifth century when the Latin Vulgate was translated and included the Apocrypha. This has been the official Bible of the Catholic church ever since, though this official decision did not silence debate during the Middle Ages. During the Reformation, Luther and Calvin put the Apocrypha aside as books good to read but not authoritative for doctrine or life. This has been the position in all Protestant churches ever since.

This dispute over the Apocrypha symbolizes much of the attitude of the Reformation. The Reformers, who demanded reliance on the Bible alone, were like the conservative "strict constructionists" today who demand that the Supreme Court interpret the Constitution exactly as its authors meant. The Catholics, on the other hand, believed that additions could be made to their basic authority, the Bible. These additions, it was claimed, did not conflict with the Bible, but added new revelation about God's will. This is like the position of the "judicial activists" who interpret the Constitution in the manner they think its authors would have decided if they had been faced with present-day issues. Conservative opponents say this is rewriting the Constitution. Likewise, the Reformers were conservatives who said that adding the Apocrypha and other Catholic writings to the Church's basic authority was really rewriting and radically changing the meaning of the Bible.

ETERNAL OR OBSOLETE?

Putting the Apocrypha aside for the moment, we must ask whether we want to include the Old Testament today at all. One scholar has said that it was inevitable that the early Church would accept the Old Testament because it had no other written authority; that it was sad that circumstances forced the Reformers to keep it; but it is tragic that we today are still proclaiming it as an authority over us.

Reasonable Opposition

The objections to the Old Testament are largely those we have seen enumerated by Jesus and the writers of the New Testament when they rejected parts of it. The Old Testament is a very ritualistic book, filled with the duties of priests and the requirements of sacrifices that have no authority over the Christian. It is also a legal book, one that specifically says, "Do this and you shall live," in direct contrast to the New Testament message, "Live by faith in Christ and you will be enabled to act as God desires you to." The vast majority of the laws of the Old Testament are of no interest to Christians, since they have to do with the civil and ritual laws of a society that is totally divorced from our own. The Old Testament is thus like the quaint old seventeenth century laws that are still on the books of many New England towns. The laws are dead letters, unenforced and unenforceable, but no one can raise interest in getting them repealed.

In a number of ways the Old Testament is not only different from Christian thought, but is opposed to it. There are passages of Israelite nationalism in which hatred for enemies is the dominant motif, a motif that is completely opposed to the spirit of Christ. There are many passages in which it is said God ordered wholesale slaughter of cities and then helped His people to achieve this goal, a view of God that is the opposite of that which we learn from the New Testament. Finally, there is no real witness to Jesus Christ in the Old Testament, for they did not know of Him, and were not able to tell what He did for mankind. On these grounds it is argued by many that we should eliminate the Old Testament from the canon, thus solving the problem of how a Christian can use it as a Christian book.

Universal Acceptance

But on the other hand, it is continually decided by the Churches that they ought to keep the Old Testament. Why? In the first place, we have the example and teaching of Jesus and the apostles. They clearly looked on the Old Testament as their authority, even with its difficulties. If we accept Jesus as our authority, then we must accept the Old Testament because He accepted it. He believed that God spoke through the Old Testament and so, it is said, can we.

Not only did Jesus and His apostles accept the Old Testament as authoritative, but so has the church ever since. Throughout the history of the church, from the earliest church council to the Presbyterian Confession of 1967, the Old Testament has been acclaimed as part of the basic document of the Christian faith. If we are to call ourselves Christians, can we oppose the united mind of the Church for two thousand years?

There are reasons for this universal acceptance of the Old Testament and it is to these we must now turn to see whether we wish to acquiesce in the decision that the Church has so often affirmed. Essentially the Old Testament is accepted because it is the indispensable background to our understanding of Jesus Christ. Christ did not come out of nowhere. He came out of the history of Israel, a history that was said to be one of God continually acting to create, redeem, and judge His people.

The New Testament claims that Christ is the fulfillment of what God had started a thousand years before when He rescued Israel from Egypt. It even claims He is the fulfillment of what God had started when He created the universe. As we look to the New Testament as the record of what God did in the first century AD, so the Old Testament is the record of what God had been doing for years before that to prepare for that consummation. The Old Testament is thus like the history of Greece and Rome, which is an indispensable source of understanding of our modern, western civilization. We cannot really understand ourselves if we fail to understand the Greeks and Romans, who are our intellectual, scientific, political, and cultural ancestors.

This is the central reason for our accepting the Old Testament. Part of the message of the New Testament is this: "In many and various ways God spoke of old to our fathers by the prophets; but in these last days he has spoken to us by a Son" (Heb. 1:1f.). If the writers of the New Testament had not had the Old Testament, they would have had to write much more than they did. It would have been necessary to tell in detail how God rescued Israel from Egypt, gave them the Promised Land, gave them a great king to keep them from danger, judged them when they revolted against Him, rescued them from Exile when they repented, and brought them back to Palestine to start again. This whole story is part of the story of Jesus Christ, for it all pointed forward to Him, promising a Great King who would come finally to redeem Israel forever.

The New Testament is thus the conclusion to a story that had already been told but was waiting for its ending. The ending makes a certain amount of sense by itself, but the authors would never have thought of publishing it by itself, because it did not give the complete picture of what they wanted to have said. In this same way, a book about politics in 20th century America assumes a number of other books, especially ones dealing with the Revolution and the Civil War which are the two major watersheds of American history.

Misplaced Arguments

The Old Testament also adds a great deal to Christian worship and understanding of life. The Psalms of the Old Testament were the songs sung by early Christians, just as they are part of our worship today. Without them our worship would be infinitely poorer. But do we have to have them canonized in order to use them in worship? We use hymns that are in no way God's word. Why should we not use Psalms that are simply good for worship in the same way?

Another argument that is used for retaining the Old Testament is the fact that it speaks in much more detail about the organized life of a nation than does the New Testament. The early Church was not a cog in the wheel of society as the Church is today, so there is little discussion in the New Testament of the way Christians are to respond to the world around them. In the Old Testament, on the other hand, there is considerable discussion of what God demands from His people in the normal course of life. It is noticeable that when today men preach sermons on social justice they often come from the Old Testament, especially from the prophets, for this was a theme that was dear to the hearts of Amos, Isaiah, and Jeremiah.

The reply that can be made to these arguments that there is much of value in the Old Testament is that there is also a great deal in the Old Testament that we don't want to follow. Israel was a theocracy, God was King, and the demands of God over His nation were issued as the law of the land. Our nations today are secular; we cannot impose God's law on those who are not willing to live by it. Thus the whole scheme of trying to describe how Christians should live today in our secular world is an almost impossible task if we are simply using the Old Testament. It always must be interpreted by the New Testament, so the latter is our real authority. Would it not be wise to make clear just what is of value to us in the Old Testament and what should be put to one side as of antiquarian interest only? Historians do this with ancient or medieval history by mainly concentrating on those events that are significant for us today. Judges and police do this by ignoring ancient laws that by common consent have become obsolete. Is not a similar process open to the Church?

REPEALING AMENDMENTS

Assuming that we agree that in some way we must continue to use the Old Testament as an authority, especially because Jesus saw it as such — how are we to decide which parts of it to use? Should we accept the whole of the Old Testament, all the books that are now in it, or should we cut it down to make it a more Christian book? We don't know for certain what the canon of the Old Testament which Jesus and His apostles used was, and as noted above, there are a number of Old Testament books that were mentioned in the New Testament.

A Proposition

Perhaps we could make the Old Testament a Christian book by eliminating the priestly laws and the civil laws and the legalistic passages. Then we could move on to eliminate the books, all of them in the latest group, "The Writings," that have been disputed for one reason or another, repealing them as the Prohibition Amendment to the Constitution was eventually repealed. Esther could be removed because it never mentions God and exhibits a vengeful nationalistic attitude. Ecclesiastes could be eliminated because it is basically a philosophical work proclaiming the vanity of existence rather than any testimony to the God of Israel. The Song of Songs should be rejected because it too has nothing to say about God, but is instead concerned about the beauties of human love and courtship. Chronicles would not be missed, it could be argued, because it is a late rewriting of the books of Samuel and Kings with an interest in describing the ritual of the temple as it was in the post-exilic period. It adds nothing to our knowledge of God's working in history. Psalms, or at least a certain number of them, ought to be deleted because they are vengeful, nationalistic and self-righteous.

If we followed this procedure, we would be left with a far more manageable book, probably one-half its present length and only a tenth of its present difficulties. Its first part would basically be a book of the history of God's dealing with His people from Creation to the time of Nehemiah, with reference made to the laws and rituals but with none of the wearying details. The second part of the work would be made up of the prophetic proclamations that are included in the works from Isaiah to Malachi. We might want to eliminate some of the prophets or parts of their sayings, but for the most part, we find them congenial to our Christian understanding of God and the way of life to which He has called us.

Roadblocks

What are the objections that can be raised to this procedure? In the first place it would be impossible to get agreement on the exact deletions to be made. No two men would agree exactly on what should be kept and what should not. Imagine what it would be like trying to get the whole Presbyterian church to agree, let alone trying to get all Protestants, or all Christians, to agree. There is general agreement now, at least among Protestants, and so there is no need to open the Pandora's box that such a procedure would entail.

But is that a sufficient reason for not trying? If we are right in our assumptions that there are parts of the Old Testament that Jesus and the apostles rejected, which are sub-Christian or anti-Christian, shouldn't it be possible to define these parts and remove them? Of course there would be disagreement, but a consensus could certainly be reached eventually to which a majority could agree. It was once thought that no form of government could ever be set up that would please the majority of a new nation, both in the beginning and for generations to come. But the United States Constitution and government have shown that to be an overly pessimistic view. Likewise agreement could be reached on a shorter, clearer, more Christian Old Testament.

The second objection is that there is no need to do this, because it is already adequately done by our preachers, teachers, and writers of curricula. We do not preach from all the parts of the Old Testament. We make selections of the parts that have something to say to us today. The curricula of church schools, when they are directly concerned with the Bible, do not deal with the passages that are of no Christian concern. Thus there is no real problem here and so pruning the canon is not a project that should be profitably taken on.

But why should this task be left to preachers, teachers, and curriculum writers? Why shouldn't the whole church decide for itself which books speak to it of God and His ways with men? Why should we place the whole bulk of the Old Testament in the hands of the neophyte who will then get lost in the midst of the "begats" and the "whole burnt offering"? A pruned Old Testament would provide direct guidance to the central message of the Old Testament for every one who opened it, instead of hiding its wheat in a sea of chaff as it does now. The Old Testament would then become the kind of authority it is meant to be, instead of being a mysterious book from the ancient history of Israel that is filled with rituals and ancient laws and nationalistic thoughts that are totally irrelevant, if not obnoxious, to the twentieth century Christian.

AN ANCIENT AND CONTINUING DEBATE

Suppose we do decide to keep the Old Testament, either in whole or in part, are we right in limiting it to the books we now have? The Roman Catholic church witnesses to the usefulness of the Apocrypha for worship and doctrine, the Eastern Orthodox church implicitly uses it for both, and the Anglican church uses it for public worship. Are we Protestants perhaps a little narrow-minded in our rejection of this set of books that has been used by most of the Church for most of its two thousand years of existence?

The Line-up

As with the Old Testament, we need not take the Apocrypha as a whole, indeed the Catholics do not include all the Apocryphal books. The books in the Apocrypha that we can probably do without are these: *First Esdras* is basically a free Greek translation of parts of Chronicles, Ezra, and Nehemiah with one extra story added. *Second Esdras* is a book written about AD 100, well after the death of Christ, and so cannot really be part of the foreshadowing of Christ. The *Additions to Esther* are stories and passages that give the book some religious content, but since the book itself is not that important, saving it by amending it is not a recommended procedure. *Tobit* and *Judith* are two books that reflect Jewish piety and devotion to the law in the period before Christ. The *Additions to Daniel* are further stories in the vein of the original book which do not add anything important to the book as it stands.

The more meaningful books are these: *The Wisdom of Solomon*, which is a book that teaches Jewish theology as it was interpreted to a Greek audience. It was perhaps known and used by Paul. The *Wisdom of Ben Sirach* is another book like Proverbs, but with a great deal of religious insight. *Baruch* speaks in the vein of Jeremiah (Baruch, in whose name the book was written, was Jeremiah's disciple) of Israel's judgment, but it is a late book, probably not being completed until after the time of Jesus. The *Prayer of Manasseh* is a cry of repentance and a prayer for forgiveness. The last two books are *First* and *Second Maccabees*. *First Maccabees* gives the history of Israel in part of the 2nd century BC, during the Maccabean revolt and restoration of the nation. The Second book covers a smaller portion of the second century, in which God's intervention in Israel's history (which is not mentioned in *First Maccabees*) is given in spectacular miraculous events.

Judgment

Do any of these books appeal to us today? None of them really deal with God's action in history from a prophetic standpoint, for prophets were not found in Israel in the time of writing of these books. The most appealing of the books is the *Wisdom of Solomon*, because it is a preview of the New Testament attempt to relate Hebrew thought to Greek readers. *First Maccabees* is perhaps next in line, but the history of the Jews in the second century is not one in which there was any clear revelation of God's way with His people. *Sirach* is probably third in importance, but it does not add anything to the theology of the Old Testament that is significant, and its prudential rules for living are of no greater significance than Proverbs. Trying to decide what books ought to be added to the Hebrew canon is similar to the task of a teacher trying to decide what books to add to an English literature reading list that already contains fifty of the greatest works. Any decision will be highly subjective and debatable, for who can define the standards of "greatness"?

Finally, when we are trying to decide what to do with the Apocrypha it is worth noting that Jesus and the first apostles probably did not know or use these books. They were found only in the Greek translation of the Old Testament (known as the Septuagint) and Jesus and His first apostles probably knew only the Hebrew Old Testament. The early Church adopted the Greek Old Testament because it was a Greek-speaking church, probably not realizing that the Hebrew Bible of Jesus was shorter than the Bible of Greek-speaking Jews. The practice of using the Apocrypha became so enshrined in the life of the Church that it was impossible to eradicate it, even when it was pointed out that in Palestine these extra books were not known. It was on the basis of these facts that Luther, Calvin, and the Protestant churches returned to the Hebrew canon of the Old Testament, rejecting the Apocrypha, and so we do to this day. Is this a debate that we wish to reopen in order to know what to say to our Roman Catholic brethren if and when we come to discuss reunion between our churches? Is this a negotiable issue, or are we determined to stand fast on our rejection of the Apocrypha?

THE NEW TESTAMENT

BIRTH AND GROWTH

The early Church did not have a New Testament. For more than one hundred and fifty years after the death of Christ, their Bible was the collection of books we now call the "Old" Testament. Only about AD 200 did the concept and the fact of a canonized New Testament come into being.

It was natural for the Church immediately after Jesus' death and resurrection to use the Old Testament as its Bible because He had done so. The Church also preserved the Sayings of Jesus, first orally, and then in written collections. The eye-witnesses to the resurrection, the apostles, were the most important authorities in the Church, and so while they lived there was no need for anything written to be used authoritatively. Paul wrote his letters to distant churches which were not reached by the eyewitnesses, or which had heretics coming in and preaching "another gospel."

Impetus

As the original apostles died, and the personal witness and authority they represented was in danger of being lost, the tradition about Jesus was written down in our four Gospels, probably by the end of the first century. Letters from church leaders were saved, especially those from Paul, because the authority they had in the first generation of the church's life was enhanced by the death of most of the witnesses. For the next one hundred years, gospels, epistles, acts, and apocalypses were written by various people in the church and were circulated, though none of them had universal authority. In the middle of the second century, however, the need for an authoritative canon became evident.

Marcion, a brilliant Christian in Rome about AD 135, decided that the Church ought to reject the Old Testament and all traces of Judaism from its faith and practice, in much the same way Hitler wanted to reject all traces of Judaism in the German Church. So Marcion collected his own canon, made up of the Gospel of Luke purged of Old Testament passages, and of ten letters of Paul, likewise purged. The Church in general reacted strongly against this limitation of the gospel and rejected Marcion and his canon. Slowly the official writings of the Church began to be recognized.

Foundation

By about AD 185 the four Gospels, as we now have them, were accepted generally as the basic element of the New Testament. Attempts at making one harmonized Gospel out of the four, or selecting one of them as the one Gospel, were rejected. The apparent reason for this rejection of a harmonized Gospel was that it would not be apostolic, for the single Gospel, even though consisting of parts of the original four, would have to be written by a later author. The differences between the Gospels were thus not felt to be sufficiently disturbing to overcome the apostolic authority of each of the four. The inclusive testimony of four witnesses was felt to be of great importance to the Church, so much so that one writer said it was inconceivable that there should be more or less. In somewhat the same way most Americans find it inconceivable that there should be more or less than three branches of government — Executive, Legislative and Judicial.

There was never an official church council that decided for four Gospels. It just happened. Other gospels were plentiful, but all were rejected and these four were given the place of honor, though at that early date they still were not quite as authoritative as the Old Testament, which was the Church's "Scripture."

Superstructural

By this same time the collection of Paul's letters had come to be accepted on about the same level as the Gospels. Marcion's rejection of the three Pastoral Epistles was not accepted, and these were kept in the collection, making thirteen letters in all. Hebrews was practically unknown in this period, and certainly was not yet believed to have been written by the Apostle Paul. Thus about AD 200 the only authoritative Christian writings were the four Gospels and the thirteen letters of Paul.

Shortly thereafter, the Acts of the Apostles was incorporated as part of the canon, accepted because it offered a bridge between the Gospels and the letters of Paul. First Peter and First John gradually came to be widely recognized and accepted in the third century, so that by AD 300 the almost universally recognized canon was four Gospels, Acts, the thirteen letters of Paul, and the Epistles of I John and I Peter. Everything else in our New Testament was disputed. This growth of the canon took place in much the same unplanned fashion that the growth of the Federal government of the United States took place. At first only basic functions like foreign relations and the postal service were federally controlled. But gradually, after considerable dispute, the government entered more and more into the daily working of the nation's economy in order to keep peace between groups and to provide stability. Each step was disputed, but gradually, Americans in general came to agree that the steps were necessary and good.

Disputed Decorations

2 Peter was disputed because it was in a very different style from 1 Peter and so probably was not by the Apostle. James and Jude were not known to be apostles and so their letters were held by many to be non-canonical. Hebrews was anonymous and so was rejected by many. 2 and 3 John were too short to be of much use, and the Elder John who wrote them apparently was not an apostle. Finally, Revelation was accepted very early by much of the Church. But when it became clear that it was too different from the Gospel of John to be written by the same author, it was rejected by many, especially in the East.

The first time that our present canon is referred to in its entirety is in AD 367 when Athanasius, the Bishop of Alexandria, and probably the most influential man in the Church at the time, published our list in an Easter letter. This does not mean that all these books were recognized by all churches, for they were not. Gradually, however, they all did come to commend themselves to the churches in all parts of the known world, so that by the beginning of the Middle Ages, about AD 500, our present New Testament canon was the universal canon of the Church. That five-hundred-year journey to agreement bears many points of resemblance to the road toward unity that Europe has traveled since the Reformation, 450 years ago. Slowly Europe is becoming united, at least in the Western part, and by the 500th anniversay of the Reformation it is possible that a United States of Europe with a single constitution will have come into existence.

UNEQUAL AUTHORITIES

Many other books, in all categories, had been scrutinized during those five centuries and found wanting. Some of them, letters written in the early part of the second century, were nearly included; and several apocalypses from that same period hovered on the edge of acceptance for a hundred years or more. Gradually, however, the use of these books by the Church, its study of them and discussion about them, brought about the consensus that we have now. Still, it was recognized by some that there were differences in value among the books in the New Testamnt, for some were early and universally recognized as canonical, others were debated for years before acceptance. Officially the Church today calls all its books equal, but practically, judged by attention given to the various books, this same kind of judgment of differences of value is made by readers and teachers today.

Pious Fictions

The first group are those accepted by AD 300: Gospels, Acts, Pauline epistles, 1 Peter, and 1 John. The rest needed pious fictions to get them in. 2 Peter was said to be by the Apostle and so accepted, though many had thought it was not by Peter. 2 and 3 John and Revelation were said to be by the Apostle John, though many had recognized that they were written by someone other than the author of the Gospel and 1 John. Hebrews was said to be Pauline and so acceptable, though there was no evidence for this and much against it. James and Jude were said to be by apostles who were identified with Jesus' brothers of those same names, though this was an extremely speculative procedure.

The truth of the matter is that these pious fictions were maintained in order to include books that the Church had become convinced ought to be included. The books had proven themselves over several centuries of use to be witnesses the Church needed as its rule or standard. The Church also thought that its books ought to be apostolic, so it made these books apostolic in name, because their teaching was apostolic already. This procedure is just like one still carried on by Oxford University. An ancient rule is that all members of the faculty must be holders of the Oxford M.A. degree. However, when the university wants to appoint an outsider to the faculty, someone without the degree, it simply grants him an honorary M.A. in order to live up to a rule that is no longer important but is too traditional to be repealed.

Luther's Challenge

The only overt challenge to the present canon of the New Testament in the later history of the Church came from that great proponent of biblical authority, Martin Luther. Luther proclaimed that the justification of the sinner through faith in Jesus Christ is the center of the gospel message, and therefore "what preaches Christ" should be the standard for deciding the proper books to include in the canon.

On this basis he rejected James, because it preached works at the expense of (though not the exclusion of) justification by faith. He rejected Hebrews because it said that Christians who had rejected the faith could never be readmitted to God's grace. He also rejected Jude and Revelation — Jude because it appears to be copied from 2 Peter and has nothing original to say about Christ, Revelation because of its obscurity and tendency towards a vindictive attitude against enemies. Thus Luther claimed that four of the seven disputed writings were not of the same value as the rest of the New Testament. Luther's relentless selectivity is like that of an efficiency expert coming into an office and demanding that an old, slow secretary be fired for the sake of proficiency, no matter what emotional ties the office staff may have to her due to her long service.

His standard, "What preaches Christ," was not very different from the standard of the early Church. The most important test was that of apostolic origin. Anything that was written by an apostle was authoritative in the Church because all the apostles were authoritative. The trouble with this criterion was that it was not elastic enough to admit all the books the Church wanted to admit to the canon. Only two of the Gospels were even said to be written by apostles (Matthew and

John), but the other two were called apostolic because they were written by apostles' companions (Mark was thought to have been Peter's interpreter; Luke was known to have accompanied Paul). As was discussed above, the problem of the other seven writings which the Church wanted to include was solved by claiming that they were all written by apostles. The question is whether, now that we are considerably more certain which books were apostolic and which were not, we should revise the canon in the light of our new knowledge.

The truth of the matter is that the books were not chosen because of their actual connections with apostles. That was the excuse used to get them in. The reason they were chosen was that they had proven themselves. They had been used by the Church for centuries and had shown themselves to be the books which best represented the apostolic witness to Christ. It is this truth of their witness that was most important. The assertion of apostolic origin was a rationalization of choices made on other grounds. It is something like the cry for "property rights" or for "law and order" in the United States today, which are sometimes rationalizations or euphemisms for "keep the black man in his place."

A CHICKEN AND ITS EGG

Does this course of events and arguments mean that the Church chose the New Testament and so is the authority over it? It is clear that there was a Church before there was a New Testament. The New Testament as we know it did not exist for three hundred years after the death of Christ, and it was certainly through the life of the Church, its councils, discussions, and worship that these books came to achieve their position. It is disputed, however, that this can be called "choosing" by the Church. It is said that the books imposed themselves, for the Church did not see itself as an authority over the books, but saw the New Testament as the authority over the Church. The New Testament canon was meant to serve as a standard for faith and life so that the Church could be judged by it. The Church "recognized" these particular writings as God's Word to it and so was willing to live under their authority. This distinction between "choosing" and "recognizing" is similar to the difference between the Revolutionary War period and our own: the writers of the Constitution "chose" those laws and rights which they decided should be binding upon the United States; we, on the other hand, "affirm" or "recognize" the Constitution as the authority over us, without being able to "choose" it.

Alterations

But are we, the Church of the twentieth century, in the same position to alter the canon as the citizens of twentieth century America are free to alter the Constitution? The Constitution is open-ended; it can be changed at any time. The canon, on the other hand, has been looked on as "closed" so that nothing can be added, because it is said that the Bible is basically a sourcebook of history, not a book of science or logic. The Bible is the witness to what God did in the past, in the history of Israel and in the life of Jesus. A witness must be someone who has first hand, or nearly first hand knowledge. Only the first generation of the Church had that knowledge, and so only the writings of the first generation can be authoritative. In just this same way only the reports of those who lived at the time can be authoritative witnesses to what happened in the Civil War.

But is it true to say that the New Testament is only a record, a witness to what God did at a certain time? Is there not a great deal of interpretation as well as straight reporting? Paul is certainly a witness to the resurrection, and so we would want to keep him as an authority. But he also draws many conclusions from the facts he knew, so why cannot the conclusions of future generations be equally as authoritative as his were?

For example, there was universal agreement of all the

branches of the Church in the fourth and fifth centuries at the two great Councils of Nicea and Chalcedon. Two creeds that are recognized by almost all the churches of the world were written by those councils. They are statements of the Trinity, of the relationship of Christ and the Holy Spirit to God, and of the human and divine in Christ Himself. These were conclusions drawn from the facts of the life and teaching of Christ as they are reproduced in the New Testament. They are conclusions that are almost universally accepted in the Church, or at least they have been up until this century. Why should they be excluded from the canon?

Interpretations

These creeds are interpretations of the meaning of Christ and as such continue the process of interpretation that had been begun in the New Testament. Not only did they continue what the apostles started, but they were able to use all the extant writings of the apostles and thus to unify their thought. In addition they were able to use three centuries of theological debate as the basis for their statement of the universal faith of the Church.

These creeds are just like a history of the Civil War written in 1965. The evidence of debate has raised most of the important issues and answered those for which evidence is available. We today have a far truer and clearer understanding of what took place in the Civil War than any of the participants did. Thus, the authorities in the Civil War and its meaning are modern historians, not the participants. In the same way the great creeds of the Church are a truer, clearer and more universal authority than any particular book of the New Testament is, because New Testament books are open to a wide variety of interpretations.

The real question that this raises is whether or not we want to draw a fine line between writings which are canonical and those that are not. The two creeds just mentioned are far more universally accepted and understood in the Church than is, for example, the Epistle of Jude. They provide a far greater witness to Christ and His meaning for mankind than does the Epistle of James. They are not much longer than the second and third Epistles of John, but they have had far more influence in the Church and continue to have that influence. For example, if and when the present Consultation on Church Union provides a Plan of Union between the main Protestant denominations, it will almost certainly contain the Creed of Nicea as one of its basic documents, for it is this creed that presents explicitly the doctrine of the Trinity.

Use and Authority

When we try to answer this question whether there should be more books, or documents, in the canon, there are a number of points that need to be considered. The first is that the Church of each generation determines its authorities by the documents it uses. This means that the great creeds are in fact more expressive of the mind of the Church universal than, is, for example, the book of Revelation, for the creeds are used more. The disputed books of the New Testament are seldom used in the Church; they are often ignored because they are not as useful in proclaiming the gospel as are the other, more central books. In this same way the Westminster Confession has come to be largely unused in the Presbyterian Church, for the Bible speaks more clearly and relevantly than does that seventeenth century document.

In practice there is a "canon within the canon." While all the books of the New Testament are canonical, some are more so than others, not officially, but practically. The Epistle to the Romans is studied, preached, read, and discussed far more than any other New Testament epistle. When a scholar is trying to think through the theology of the New Testament he goes to Romans as one of his chief sources. Likewise the Gospels, often one more than another, are the other primary source for understanding the meaning of the New Testament. The conclusions that are drawn from other books must be measured by these central books. As in any group of equal authorities, whether human or parchment, some are always more equal than others.

In practice, therefore, the authorities of the Church go just about in this order: Jesus, as His teachings are given in the Synoptic Gospels; Paul; John as he understands Christ in his Gospel and First Epistle. After that we come to the lesser authorities, Hebrews first, and then on down the line. Somewhere about the level of Hebrews the Creeds of Nicea and Chalcedon enter in as authorities. It is not usually said officially that this is so, but this is the practice of much of the Church.

Conclusion

The particular collection of books that is found in our canon is the heritage that we have received from our forefathers in the Church. The Old Testament was gradually collected over a period ranging from 600 BC to AD 90. The last books were continually disputed, and even are today, for Catholics and Protestants disagree. The New Testament began to be collected around AD 50 to 60 when Jesus' sayings were written down, but it took another four hundred years before the Church universally accepted the present canon.

In neither case was there a clear theological standard by which the two sets of books were all judged. The collections were a matter of history, of generations of sifting by the Church as it found what books truly conveyed God's Word to it. There was no modern sophistication in the Church's attitude, for every book was accepted or rejected as a whole. We today would be inclined to exercise a little editorial discretion in order to eliminate the points of controversy that were raised by some of the books. They, on the other hand, ignored difficulties by giving them allegorical interpretations that suppressed the literal meaning.

Today the Church must face the fact that modern man knows that knowledge increases immensely each year. Is the Church to say that in the area of Christian faith there has been nothing new in two thousand years? Are we to imply that all the work that has gone into theology in the last one hundred years has paid no dividends because we still depend solely upon the Bible of the early Church as our Bible? Perhaps the time has come for the Church to make some changes. Elimination of some Old Testament books and the possible addition of one or more from the Apocrypha would be a start. Critical scrutinizing of the seven hotly debated New Testament books would come next. Finally the addition of some of the universally accepted Creeds, especially that of Nicea, and possibly the one written at Chalcedon, would be an excellent third step.

God acted in Israel and the Church to preserve and enhance the authority of those books which truly witnessed to Him. It can be plausibly claimed in the light of modern knowledge, which also is God-given, that some other books were included without that full justification. The Church is not bound to the latter. The churches of the Reformation began their existence by paring the Bible's limits, and so will be certainly in character if they continue that same process.

4

The Inerrant Bible of Fundamentalism

BACKGROUND AND BIRTH

Fundamentalism claims to be two thousand years old. It is in fact a modern phenomenon, though it has some roots in the thought of Jesus and the New Testament, as do all Christian theological viewpoints. Its most direct ancestor in its view of the Bible is post-Reformation theology. That theology had lost the flexibility and genius of the great Reformers, Luther and Calvin, while attempting to continue their thought.

The First One Thousand Years

For one thousand years between the Church's agreement on the Canon of the Bible and its Reformation division over the meaning of the Bible, the Allegorical Method of interpreting the Scriptures was in vogue. By this method, scholars unwilling to admit that the Bible had difficulties, could explain away the importance of the literal meaning of any passage, by giving it a "spiritual" or allegorical meaning. By this means all the difficulties in the Bible were dealt with. For example, the Old Testament commands concerning sacrifices were reinterpreted to mean spiritual exercises, like prayer or giving money to the Church.

In the same way as Stalin said, "The constitution means

what I say it means," the Church became the master of Scripture. It could read into the Bible anything it pleased. And so the medieval Church justified indulgences, prayer to the saints, and Purgatory. When Luther learned what the Bible literally said, he opposed much medieval theology, because he saw that it went against the literal meaning of the Bible.

The Bible was Luther's authority. But so was his Christian conscience and reason, for he believed that there were errors in the Bible and that some books were of secondary value. The living Christ, known by faith, was Luther's primary authority, but the Bible shared this authority when it witnessed to Christ. Calvin was a little more reticent about downgrading books of the Bible, but he did recognize errors in it. Centrally, however, Calvin stressed that the Holy Spirit inspired the biblical writers so that they wrote God's Word to man. Luther was a typical German genius, one who had brilliant insights which he then overstated. Calvin, like his neutral Switzerland caught between great nations, was more cautious, and was thus able to present a somewhat more balanced view.

Ancestors and Antagonists

In the post-Reformation period there was a hardening of theological lines. The Catholics stressed the absolute authority of the Pope, and in response Protestants stressed the absolute authority of the Bible. Calvin had spoken of the Holy Spirit's inspiration. This was later taken to mean, in opposition to Calvin's own thought, that the Spirit had controlled the writing of the Bible to ensure that it was free from all error. For two centuries this was the dominant Protestant view, for all who disagreed with it usually left the Church.

At the beginning of the nineteenth century, however, there arose modern literary and historical criticism which were applied to the Bible in order to find its original meaning.

Accompanying modern criticism was theological Liberalism, which rejected the supernaturalism of the Bible along with most of the central tenets of the biblical faith. Thus, in many people's minds rejection of the inerrant Bible (which is basic to modern criticism) meant a rejection of historic Christianity.

This, as we shall see, was guilt by association, for biblical criticism does not necessarily lead to a rejection of the historic faith of the Church. In the present day the same sort of guilt by association is seen in the attitude of those who object to economic socialism because it arose in the modern world in connection with totalitarian Communism. The experience of Britain and Sweden, free and democratic socialist nations having socialist economies, makes it clear that it is false to believe that socialism inevitably leads to Communism. Likewise it is false to think that biblical criticism inevitably leads to Liberalism.

Defenders of the Faith

Fifty years ago, however, it was not at all clear that there was an essential difference between modern criticism and Liberalism. In reaction to Liberalism there arose in the early twentieth century a movement called "Fundamentalism" which aimed at defending the historic faith of the Church against the anti-supernaturalism of the Liberals. The movement's name developed from the desire to present the "fundamentals" of Christianity. These were variously delineated, but always included one plank in the platform that opposed biblical criticism. This Fundamental asserted the inspiration, infallibility, and inerrancy of the Bible which was "God's Word."

The reason for studying this viewpoint is that it objects to the use of literary and historical tools to understand the original meaning of the Bible. If Fundamentalism is true, then all modern investigation of the Bible is false, and indeed sinful. If on the other hand, the Fundamentalist theory of the Bible is erroneous, then the way is open to assess the value of various methods used to interpret the Bible. Fundamentalism is thus a mountain barrier that must be crossed if the traveler wishes to come into the world of modern theology. This chapter will attempt to go over the top rather than ignoring it by going around the side.

Of course there are a variety of Fundamentalists, so there are differing opinions and arguments about specific subjects. Some arguments are very sophisticated, some are less so. In this chapter we will be dealing with one of the most erudite of the group, Dr. J. I. Packer, an Anglican theologian who has written a book entitled *Fundamentalism and the Word of God* (published in the United States by the William B. Eerdman Publishing Company, Grand Rapids, Michigan). It is this book that we will be considering and using as the basis for our discussion. Most of his arguments, though not all, would be accepted by those who look on the Bible as the inerrant Word of God, so we shall not be far wrong in using his thought as typical.

THE WHOLE TRUTH AND NOTHING BUT

Every Last Word

The basic principle of Fundamentalism is that "the teaching of the written Scriptures is the Word which God spoke and speaks to His Church, and is finally authoritative for faith and life. To learn the mind of God, one must consult His written Word. What Scripture says, God says. The Bible is inspired in the sense of being word-for-word God-given." (Packer, p. 47). The crucial principle here is that every word of the Bible was "spoken" by God and is to be accepted by Christians as the absolute rule for faith and life, as much as if God Himself appeared and spoke to us personally today. As Dr. Spock's *Baby and Child Care* is word-for-word the representation of Dr. Spock's thought, so the Bible is exactly the expression of the mind of God.

Since the whole Bible is the Word of God, it is infallible and inerrant. The adjective "infallible" means to say that the Bible is never deceiving or misleading, but may be taken as it stands as completely trustworthy and reliable, for God is completely reliable. "Inerrant" means that the Bible is completely true, for it is the message of God, who cannot make errors. This inerrancy applies not only to ideas, but to the very words themselves, for the Bible is "verbally inspired." "Words signify and safeguard meaning; the wrong word distorts the intended sense. Since God inspired the biblical text in order to communicate His Word, it was necessary for him to ensure that the words written were such as did in fact convey it" (89).

The authority of the words is important because the Bible consists of "revealed truths." Revelation is held to be "propositional," a revelation of propositions and assertions, rather than primarily a "personal" revelation of God Himself. Since men did not fully know who Christ was or what the meaning of His life, death and resurrection was from simply observing Him, it was necessary for God to reveal this meaning to the writers of the New Testament. The apostles could not simply be witnesses who reported what they saw and heard, because they were not able to see the whole truth about Christ. Therefore, they had to have the truth revealed to them by a communication from God.

This understanding of what the Bible is, contains within it many implications about the problem which man faces and the means by which God can solve this problem. It says that a substantial amount of man's problem is intellectual, that he needs information like that in text books. It says that by means of this true information man can be changed. This is similar to the point of view that a man can be educated by books and machines, even without personal contact with teachers. The opposing viewpoint of most modern theology is that man does not need information primarily, but needs to meet God personally in order to be changed. In the same way a pupil needs the inspiration, enthusiasm, dedication, and personal involvement of teachers if he is ever going to be educated. Fundamentalism does not deny the need for personal involvement, but its intellectual understanding of the Bible greatly plays it down.

The Controlling Hand

God created His inerrant Word by the work of the Holy Spirit, by inspiration. "Inspiration is to be defined as a supernatural, providential influence of God's Holy Spirit upon the human authors which caused them to write what He wished to be written for the communication of revealed truth to others" (77). Fundamentalists take pains to say that this does not imply a mechanical dictation by God to human authors, for it is clear that there is in the Bible a wide variety in vocabulary, style, and emphasis. They also say that there was not necessarily any unusual state of mind involved in inspiration, indeed the inspired authors may not have known that they were inspired. God "adapted His inspiring activity to the cast of mind, outlook, temperament, interests, literary habits and stylistic idiosyncrasies of each writer" (79).

The basic assumption is that human writers need not make mistakes if God does not wish it. The analogy they use is that there is no reason why human beings must be sinful, if, as in the case of Christ, God intends them to be perfect. God simply acted to "overrule sinful human writers so that they wrote nothing but what He intended" (80). But this does not mean that the writers were robots. Rather, "their thinking and writing was *both* free and spontaneous on their part *and* divinely elicited and controlled, and what they wrote was not only their own work but also God's work" (80).

In this picture of the working of God in the actual writing down of the Bible, there is something similar to the guiding hand of a teacher as a pupil is learning to write. When the child is at the stage where he knows most of the letters, but occasionally makes mistakes, his hand is allowed to be free within the loose grip of the teacher's as long as the letters are made correctly. But when the child begins to make a mistake, the teacher stops his hand to prevent it. In this way the child's correct writing is "free and spontaneous," but whenever a mistake looms up, the teacher "controls" it to make the writing "inerrant." God's control of man's mind in the Fundamentalist theory is of course much more complex, but the basic idea is the same, over-ruling man and preventing him from making mistakes.

This is the position that Fundamentalists generally hold with regard to Scripture. Most of it holds together so well that the theory has to be accepted or rejected as a whole. It is a complete view of the way God works (or worked) in the life of man, of what we need to know about God, of how He revealed Himself, and of what we are supposed to do with discrepancies in the Bible. It is all tied up in the one central thought: The Bible is the Inerrant Word of God. Fundamentalists claim that their view is the teaching of the Old Testament, of Jesus, of the Apostles, and of the Church universal until the nineteenth century. They go even further and say that denial of this view of Scripture involves the denial of the whole of Christianity. Let us look at the evidence.

CLAIMED FOUNDATIONS

One story in the Old Testament describes the Ten Commandments Moses received as being engraved on two stone tables "written with the finger of God" (Ex. 31:18). It is claimed that "the rest of the Pentateuch, and the later prophetic passages . . . were always regarded as no less divine, no less truly words of God, than the words which God had written with His own finger" (53). The assertion contained in this "always" is not proven. It is exactly this dispute over the authority of the Old Testament that we took up in an earlier chapter in which we discussed Jesus' and the Apostles' teaching. The teaching of the Jewish rabbis is somewhat shadowy, for we have little direct evidence of theories about the Bible's authority for the Jews of Jesus' day.

The Temptation of Wishful Thinking

We do have direct evidence from the New Testament, however, and here also the Fundamentalists claim that this evidence supports them. It is claimed that Christ "confirmed the absolute authority of the Old Testament for others and submitted to it unreservedly Himself" (55). There follows a series of statements which we discussed in chapter 1 in which Jesus affirmed the Old Testament. The statements in which He challenged the Old Testament, however, are explained away as His "disentangling principles of the Mosaic law from the perversions of scribal" interpretation (56). Rather than challenging the letter of the law, He is said to have "challenged current interpretations of Scripture, but shared and endorsed the accepted view of its nature and status as an authoritative utterance of God" (58). The evidence amassed in chapter one of this book makes it abundantly clear that Fundamentalists read their own view into the teaching of Jesus, missing completely the opposition that He showed to parts of the Old Testament.

Reading a set of documents so as to make them agree with our own position is a temptation that every reader faces. This problem arises most insistently when there is a tradition of two diametrically opposed views so that all participants in the debate are supposed to be on one side or the other. Fundamentalists see this as a black-and-white dispute bewteen the "modernists" who see no authority in the Bible, and themselves who call the Bible inerrant. Fundamentalists can easily then claim Jesus for their side. But Jesus is on neither side, for that modern dichotomy was not the only choice in His day. He stands between them and so His view is rejected or ignored by both sides.

This problem of black-or-white positions comes up constantly in political life when men are deeply divided. In parts of the United States today where the races are rigidly opposed, anyone who attempts to reconcile the two sides is misunderstood and so has his view rejected. One side demands civil disobedience, the other side calls for imposition of a police state. Those who seek a positive solution are called "Uncle Toms" or "spineless liberals." By standing between the two camps they are understood by neither, but they do have the ennobling (there being no other aristocracy in America) possibility of becoming martyrs.

Fundamentalists believe that they demonstrate their theory of inerrancy when they point to two passages we have previously discussed, Matthew 5:17-19 and 2 Timothy 3:16. We saw that both these passages refer only to the Old Testament and so cannot be used to speak of the whole Bible. In addition they do not say what the Fundamentalist claims they say.

When Matthew says, "Not an iota, not a dot, will pass from the law until all is accomplished," he is not saying that the Old Testament is inerrant in all its remarks. He is saying that Christ is the fulfillment of the whole of the Old Testament, for it points towards Him and prophesies His coming.

Likewise in 2 Timothy 3:16, "All scripture is inspired by God," there is no grounds for saying that God can inspire only inerrant Scripture. "Inspired" means, "Inbreathed by the Holy Spirit," and just as Christians who have received the Holy Spirit still sin, so also Scripture that has been inspired by the Holy Spirit can still be in error in part. The central point of inspiration is not that these writings have no errors, but that Scripture does convey to us what God intends us to know.

Apostolic Humility

A certain amount of authority lay in the Old Testament,

but the apostles also claimed authority for themselves, as we saw in chapter 2. There is no denying that they thought they spoke on the authority of Christ at times, and at other times spoke on their own authority as witnesses to God's action in Christ. But we also saw that there were times when the apostles realized that their opinions were only their opinions and not equally authoritative with the Word of the Lord. The difficulty that this raises for our understanding of the authority of Paul, for example, is not dealt with by Packer. Undoubtedly, the answer would be that even though Paul was giving his own opinion and not a command from the Lord, yet his own opinion was still the Word of God because of his apostolic authority. Can we accept something that is "no command of the Lord" as still necessarily the absolute truth of God? It still may be authoritative to us, but it is difficult to see how Paul's authority can be equated with Christ's as Packer claims: "Apostolic utterances are the truth of Christ and possess the authority of Christ; they are to be received as words of God, because what they convey is, in fact, the word of God" (64). Paul knew the difference between his own words and the authority of Christ, but Paul's words on this matter are basically ignored by Fundamentalists.

The humility of the Apostle Paul in this matter is a striking departure from the normal human tendency of second generation leaders to claim that their own views are identical with those of the original founder. In the years following the death of President John Kennedy, many people who had been close to him claimed that they spoke in his name. For example, some opponents of the Vietnam War claimed that John Kennedy's view was their own, that the United States should never send infantry into an Asian war. Paul could have claimed the authority of Jesus for everything he said, so his refusal to do this indicates how vastly higher Paul rated Jesus' teaching than his own.

Inspired Mistakes

Not only do Fundamentalists claim that the apostles agreed with their view of the Bible, but they also assert that the post-apostolic Church held a Fundamentalist view. Packer knows that the subject of inerrancy was not discussed in the early Church. He assumes, instead, that "inspiration" and "inerrancy" mean the same thing, which is not true.

His understanding is that what "the Church believed itself to be doing was not creating the New Testament, but recognizing it. God was held to have created it, by inspiring the books destined to compose it; the Church sought merely to discern which books those were" (66). Saying that the Bible is "inspired" is not at all the same as saying it is "inerrant," for most Christians think that the Bible is inspired in some way by God, but do believe it contains some errors.

This is an absolutely crucial distinction. The word, "Inspired," is used of writers, poets, artists, and preachers to indicate that the results of their work go beyond normal human expectations. For a Christian this means that God Himself is the "Spirit" who "inspires." An inspired man has been given insight and ability to communicate his insight so that others can share it, and this for the Christian is how God is at work in all realms of life. The apostles were inspired in their preaching and writing, for they were given a deep insight into God's presence and action in Jesus, and this they wrote.

But insight does not preclude error. Inspiration provides something new, but it does not eliminate all that is old. So in anything that is inspired, it is the responsibility of the listener or viewer to discern what is inspired and what is merely the old framework in which the inspiration is presented. Inspiration does not eliminate error. Thus, when the word, "inspired," is used in Christian writings, it can only be equated with "inerrant" when the writer explicitly says so. The Bible and the early Church never make such an equation.

The truth of the matter is that it cannot be said that Jesus or the apostles in their acceptance of the authority of the Old Testament ever made a claim that it was inerrant, though they did believe and state that it was inspired. There is no clear discussion in the New Testament or in the early Church on the subject of the inspiration of the Bible, whether it is infallible and inerrant, or whether it should be spoken of as "the words of God." This was not a central issue in the early Church, and did not arise as an issue of central importance until after the Reformation. Throughout the Middle Ages the Church had been the supreme authority and so only a few individual scholars such as Augustine thought deeply about the Bible's inspiration. When the Bible became the supreme authority, during the Reformation, then the debate started. The question each reader must decide is whether or not the Fundamentalists are right in the claim that their view of the Bible was the view held by Jesus, the apostles, and the early Church.

THE SINFULNESS OF OPPONENTS

Not only do Fundamentalists present and defend their own position, but they also point out what they think are the weaknesses of their opponents' position. They think that those who do not accept their position (called "liberals") have rejected historic Christianity as it is proclaimed in the New Testament and as it has been basically believed throughout the history of the Church universal.

A Multitude of Images

The reasoning behind this charge is as follows: the Bible is the one and only measure of truth. Reason must be used only to understand it, not to decide where it is authoritative and where it is not. "If the human mind is set up as the measure and test of truth, it will quickly substitute for man's incomprehensible Creator a comprehensible idol fashioned in man's own image; man wants a god he can manage and feel comfortable with, and will inevitably invent one if allowed" (171). Biblical criticism thus inevitably leads to idolatry.

This charge completely misunderstands the Bible and biblical criticism, which will be discussed in detail in the rest of this book. Fundamentalists misunderstand the Bible because they think it has one view of God which any man accepting the Bible's authority will be able to see. The first two chapters of Genesis are almost enough in themselves to disprove this theory because God is seen so differently in the two accounts of Creation. Certainly the God of War described in parts of the Old Testament cannot be easily combined with the God of Love found in other parts of the Old Testament, and in all the New Testament.

If there is to be a single understanding of God taken from the Bible, it must come by the synthesizing power of man's mind and not simply by acceptance of the Bible. Not even Fundamentalists can escape this quagmire because the Bible has a great many images and metaphors used of God that can only be interpreted by human reasoning.

Interpreting what God is like from the numerous word pictures given of Him in the Bible is like trying to determine who was to blame for World War I. There is general agreement over what happened; the facts are fairly clear. But interpretation of those facts is disputed: there have been historians who blamed the Germans, and they have been opposed by others who blamed all the great nations equally. The facts do not speak for themselves in that War, any more than they do in the Bible's witness to God, or to Jesus.

Fashioning Idols

Jesus' attitude towards the Old Testament was discussed in our first chapter and was seen to be ambiguous. In the next chapter it was asserted that Jesus claimed absolute authority over men Himself. A simple summary of this would be to say that Jesus is our primary authority, the Bible is not, but must be judged in the light of Him. This view is called "idolatry" by Packer. He makes this charge on the grounds that Christ did not set Himself up as the judge over Scripture. "The Christ of the New Testament and of history . . . does not judge Scripture; He obeys it and fulfills it" (61). A Christ who places Himself as an authority over Scripture "is a Christ of human imagination, made in the theologian's own image . . . If the construction of such a Christ is not a breach of the second commandment, it is hard to see what is . . . to worship a Christ who did not receive Scripture as God's unerring word, nor require His followers to do so, would seem to be idolatry in the strictest sense" (62).

Who is constructing an imaginary Christ? If the biblical theologians are right in saying that Christ proclaimed Himself the supreme authority over His followers, supreme even over the Bible, then the Fundamentalists are the constructors of a false image. Indeed, they are guilty of setting up a human book over the divine Christ and so are guilty of the worship of the Bible, "Bibliolatry," as it has been called.

Protestants agree that the Bible is to be the primary written authority in the Church, but the Bible must be understood as God has given us eyes to see. Christ is not entombed in Scripture so that the only way He can rule is through this ancient book. If the New Testament is right, He is Risen, He is alive today, and governs His people through the Holy Spirit as much as through the Bible. To say Christ is Lord means to be subservient to the living Christ, not simply to the witness to Him that is found in the Bible. The Bible is like a set of instructions written by an obstetrician for his patients. The written word is his word, yet it is over-simplified and does not possess the whole authority of the doctor himself who can and may overrule his instructions in a crisis.

Father or Puppeteer?

A third charge made by Fundamentalists is that "Liberal-ism denies the rule of the Creator over His world" (161). Biblical critics are held to say that God "could not help mis-understandings and untruths creeping into the minds of His prophets and records of His revelation, because He had to take human material as He found it" (162). Undoubtedly, there are theologians who say this, but this is not necessarily typical of most biblical theologians. More often it is not said that God "could not" prevent untruths and errors, but that He simply "did not." It is a question of the way God operates in the word that is at issue here. Does God operate in the world to overrule the decisions and capabilities of men, or doesn't He?

There is no conclusive evidence from the Bible that God acted as a supernatural error-prevention supervisor when He sent His prophets. In fact, there is a continuing argument among scholars as to what exactly the prophets thought of themselves. They knew that they proclaimed the Word of God, but never said that every single word they spoke was the exact word God had given them. Other theories of how God inspired prophets are tenable on the basis of Old Testament evidence. We do not see men or women today who are abso-lutely infallible and inerrant, which prompts the conclusion that probably God does not overpower completely the weak-nesses, limitations, and errors of His people.

The truth appears to be exactly the opposite, that the sov-ereign Creator of the world acts not primarily through over-whelming power, but through weakness, the weakness like that of the Cross. At one time it was thought that the correct ana-logy for understanding God's action in the world was of an infinite force that overwhelms finite forces. Recently, it has come to be seen that this denies the essential facts given in the Bible about God and man — that they are personal. One person cannot be overwhelmed by the power of another without their relationship, and gradually their very nature, ceasing to be personal.

Thus it has come to be seen that God's love means that He implores, persuades, appeals to and draws man, as human love does. It cannot overwhelm without ceasing to be love. Thus God acts in man through the restraint and weakness of love, which allows mistakes, but in the long run is far more powerful than an overwhelming force. Parents of adolescents experience this. Parents have the power to force compliance to their wishes for a certain number of years. But children grow out of those years. The only lasting power is a loving involvement that helps children become themselves by allowing them to make mistakes. God apparently acts the same way, for He too is a Father; but the Fundamentalist theory of a divine control of biblical writers denies His loving restraint.

Intellectual Pride

Fundamentalism goes further still and calls the use of biblical criticism an example of impenitence and pride: "Repentance . . . is the abandoning of the sinful quest for intellectual autonomy and the recognition that true wisdom begins with a willingness to treat God's Word as possessing final authority" (161). Thus if a person sees the Bible as God's Word to man mediated through fallible, errant words of men which must be critically sifted, this is called impenitence, a refusal to repent and turn to Christ, which is the only way to acceptance with God. "Repentance means renouncing the pride which would hail man as the measure of all things, and embracing the humility of the little child who knows his ignorance, wants to learn and is ready to be taught. But subjectivism (i.e. biblical criticism), which makes human judgment the arbiter of divine truth, is just an expression of this pride. Its persistence in Christians is as much a besetting sin as any weakness of conduct" (161).

One of the ways in which this pride is said to manifest itself is in a perversion of the gospel of grace, which proclaims that man's salvation comes wholly as a gift from God. "Christians are tempted to pander to their pride by trying to find a way in which, after all, they can contribute something to their own salvation." One of the ways of doing this is by "explicating and qualifying God's revealed truth" (172). In trying to hear God's Word in the midst of the words of Scripture the biblical critic and the lay Christian are charged with trying "to do for ourselves what Christ has done for us already. Christ located the utterance of God for us once and for all; it is Scripture, as such." Those who do not accept this view are said to discount "the perfection and truth of Scripture in order to make room for man to contribute his own ideas to his knowledge of God" (173).

There is no doubt that there have been exhibitions of pride by biblical critics. This was especially true in the nineteenth century when some men said, "This is the 19th century, the modern world; there is nothing of consequence that we can learn from a book that is 1800 years old." In the twentieth century, however, much more humility has crept into biblical scholarship, for it is now recognized that the Bible has much of importance to say to even the most modern of men. No longer does biblical criticism imply a deaf ear turned to what the Bible proclaims.

The opposite is true, for the most prominent efforts of biblical scholarship are attempts to find as nearly as possible what the writers of the Bible really meant. Scholars are using their minds not as means of substituting their own viewpoint for the Bible's, but to make the Bible's viewpoint clear, even if it differs from their own. It is not pride to use our minds to the best of our ability, because God has given us minds and the obvious task of using them.

Indeed, at the present time there is as much pride exhibited by Fundamentalists as by others: Fundamentalists claim that their own theological heritage is the true one, that they do not have to seek what the Bible says on its main subjects because they already know. Their theological heritage is as historically conditioned as any other, however, so they will have to learn that the Bible's depths are far greater than anyone has so far plumbed.

The Fundamentalist attack on the use of the mind to discern the true meaning and history of the Bible is an attempt to seek intellectual security in a changing and ambiguous world where there can be no such security. Christians are called to live by faith in the unseen Christ, not by sight as Fundamentalists desire.

While biblical criticism has at times been an expression of sinful pride, Fundamentalism is usually an expression of sinful anxiety, a search for intellectual certainty when God has offered us instead the personal certainty of His own presence.

The difference between Fundamentalists and others at this point is similar to the difference between conservative and liberal political forces in the United States. Conservative forces are fairly satisfied with the *status quo.* They are more eager to "bear those ills we have, than fly to others we know not of," especially since it is usually someone else in the community that has most of the ills.

Liberals, on the other hand, refuse to accept the present circumstances but try in a variety of ways to change them. Sometimes they raise unfulfillable hopes that lead to trouble, but they believe this is the price that must be paid if solutions are eventually going to be found. Likewise biblical critics recognize the difficulties of interpreting the Bible, and so refuse to accept the *status quo.* They are willing to accept the chance of occasional erroneous and prideful misinterpretation, knowing that only in seeking and moving will a solution be found to the question, "What is God saying to us through the Bible?"

Mutilated Manuscripts

Fundamentalism attempts to guard its flanks by presenting answers to a variety of charges that are levelled against it. They admit that there is a slight difficulty for their position in the fact that all the manuscripts of the Bible that have been preserved have errors in them. Talk about an inerrant Bible is a theory that comes up against the hard fact that there is no example of an error-free manuscript.

This means that there is no way of telling what the actual words of God were in the original. "But faith in the consistency of God warrants an attitude of confidence that the text is sufficiently trustworthy not to lead us astray" (90). Since God intended the Scriptures to reveal the way to salvation, "It is a safe inference that He never permits them to become so corrupted that they can no longer fulfill" this purpose (90).

Besides this trust in God there is the undisputed fact that none of the manuscripts are corrupt enough so that any point of doctrine is at issue among them. But some of the facts are in dispute. For example, is the story of Jesus and the woman taken in adultery (John 8:1-11) a part of the original version of the Gospel? It is found in only one of the four major manuscripts and so may or may not be original. This story does affect the picture of Jesus given in the Gospel, for it portrays Him implicitly rejecting a Mosaic law in order to be forgiving. We cannot be certain whether to accept the story or not. Fundamentalists, like everyone else, have to live with the fact of errors in the texts. It is not quite clear, therefore, why they need to claim there were once original inerrant documents if the documents we now have are admittedly corrupt. Apparently, God is able to reveal Himself to us through the erroneous documents we have. Would He not have been able to do the same if the original writings had mistakes? We poor, weak, human beings are able to reveal ourselves to distant friends in erroneous, prejudiced letters, so it would be a wonder if the God of all could not do the same through His prophets and scribes.

Biblical Contradictions

A second charge made against Fundamentalists is that they ignore the facts that scientific criticism of the Bible has brought out during the last one hundred years. For the Fundamentalist, however, these "facts" are not facts at all: "These assured results of modern criticism' are simply popular hypotheses built on the inadmissible assumption that there may be untrue statements in Scripture" (141). Clearly the assumption of Fundamentalism is that there are no untrue statements in Scripture. It is impossible that there be any errors, and so anything that looks like an error must be otherwise explained.

Differences between the various accounts of the Gospels are harmonized, that is, an explanation is developed to show that there is no discrepancy, but both reports are true. When only strained or artificial expedients can harmonize biblical discrepancies, it is said that the present state of knowledge is inadequate to explain the problem, the supposition being that in the future it may become possible. Thus the conclusion that the two writers disagree so that only one of them can be right is rejected even if there is no alternative explanation offered (110). This desire to bring peace and harmony is reminiscent of Solomon's offer to divide a disputed baby in two to settle the contradictory claims of the two women involved. This solution says that they both were right. The result would be a certain kind of harmony, but it would destroy the life of the baby. Likewise in some differences between biblical writers there is no viable middle way, so one or the other must be chosen as true.

Scientific Method

The charge that harmonizing is abdicating reason and not

being intellectually honest is also rejected. Scientific criticism, when it is the name given to the various forms of biblical criticism, is said to be an "irrelevant testimony to one's own prejudices" (129) and "uncritical muddle-headedness" (130). The reason given for this conclusion is that real "scientific criticism for the Christian must mean the effort to understand and appreciate Scripture *as what it is* — God's truth in writing. Such criticism is an exercise of reasoning faith. But to subject Scripture to a scientific critical technique designed to help us tell true from false among fallible human records would be an act of unbelief that was both unscientific and uncritical, for that would be treating Scripture as something other than it is" (129f.).

This is the heart of the matter. All Christians agree that scientific criticism means treating the Bible as what it is. It is certainly, as Packer asserts, unscientific to treat anything as if it were something other than it is. Approaching a computer textbook as if it were a novel would mean that the wrong techniques would be used to analyze it and an erroneous judgment made concerning its value. Trying to understand a man as if he were only an animal would mean missing what is distinctively human and so would produce an unscientific anthropology.

The crucial question then is: what is the Bible? Fundamentalists claim that it is basically a textbook of theological doctrines that must either be accepted or rejected. The rest of this book will show that that is far too simplistic an answer, and is therefore in error. The Bible is literature, and so must be approached with literary assumptions, questions, and tools. But it is also history, and so must also be viewed with the eyes of the historian. But above all it is a personal witness by many men to the presence and action of God in their lives, and so it must also be understood as a book of theological images. It is not a book of doctrines, but a book of images that must be collected and interpreted to serve as the basis for doctrines.

The proof of this viewpoint, other than the objections already raised against Fundamentalism, is to be found in the attempt of the next five chapters to deal with the Bible as if it had this variety of characteristics. The test of this bridge to understanding will only come as we walk on it.

EVALUATION

True Experience

Fundamentalists usually arrive at their understanding of the Bible by two roads, through experience and through training. In reading the Bible they come to hear God speaking to them through it. They read, for example, "You shall love your neighbor as yourself" and something within them responds to that call and says, "Yes, that is the way men ought to live." Explaining this as "God speaking" to them means to say, "I have learned here something that seems to me to be absolutely true, so absolute that only God Himself could be the guarantee of it."

All Christians have experienced a new insight into reality that has come to them from the Bible, and usually they have called this "God's Word" to them. The Fundamentalists, therefore, have grasped an essential fact, that the Bible is in some way God's Word to those who will listen. If a choice had to be made between Fundamentalists and those who said the Bible is merely a record of man's religious pilgrimage, there is no doubt that Fundamentalists are much closer to the truth of Christian experience.

False Conclusion

The error in Fundamentalism arises when their true Christian experience is taken beyond its reasonable limits. The fact that God does speak to man through the Bible is taken to mean that the whole Bible is God's Word to man and is inerrant because He does not make mistakes. That is simply not a logical deduction to make from the experience.

No one knows by experience that every word of the Bible comes to him as a communication from God. This is a theory that Fundamentalists learn from each other. That is where the error enters in. A Fundamentalist's experience in reading the Bible is similar to that of other Christians and provides a true foundation for beginning to talk about the Bible. But the training of Fundamentalists is false, for it imposes a simplistic view of the Bible when a far more complex one is needed.

Flat Earth Complex

Fundamentalism is a partial truth that had value before modern criticism arose, for it truly stressed that the Bible is the means by which God speaks to men. When modern criticism, literary, historical, and theological, began to assert its influence in the nineteenth century, it became clear that just calling the Bible God's inerrant Word was an oversimplification. That theory was like the ancient view that the world was flat: the world appears flat and can be assumed to be so for most practical purposes of day-to-day living. New insight made it clear, however, that for some purposes such as space flight, travelling and understanding the universe, recognition of the earth's roundness, which is not immediately obvious, is essential.

In a similar way a simple view of the Bible, which comes from immediate Christian experience, is of value for reading it daily and listening for God to speak through it. But for a full understanding, it is essential that Christians know that the Bible is a complex library of books that can be properly understood only if the very best tools and assumptions are used in the effort. Some of those tools and assumptions now need to be discussed.

5

The Literature of the Bible

The Bible is not only a divine book, but it is at the same time a very human book. It is theological in content, but literary in form. The Bible is literature. It is not a scientific treatise or a textbook of doctrine. Rather, it is literature, and therefore can best be understood as other works of literature are understood. In this chapter we will show what kind of literature the Bible is and how literary criticism can aid in bringing out God's Word, which the Bible is also.

CRITICISM AS EVALUATION

The word "criticism" is a difficult word for Christians to accept in connection with the Bible, their primary written authority. Normally the word "criticism" today is used to mean, "Showing what is wrong," but that is only negative criticism. Positive criticism is something substantially different. If a synonym for it were to be given, "evaluation" would be appropriate.

Positive criticism is the attempt to evaluate the material in question, asking and answering the pertinent questions that will enable the true meaning of the material to emerge. The main goal and result of Biblical Criticism in its various forms is not debunking the Bible, but understanding it. Sometimes it must be said that statements of author or date or event are probably in error, but that is only a subsidiary result of the central goal of understanding. Biblical Criticism is like the restoration of a great painting: dirt and shellac must be removed from the painting, changing our view of it somewhat, in order to let the old master speak for himself.

Biblical Criticism is a rope made of four closely intertwined strands. The first strand is Textual Criticism in which the vast multitude of ancient handwritten texts are compared in order to recreate the original as closely as we can. Next comes Literary Criticism, which uses the techniques applied to other literature in order to answer how books were written, by whom, and what kinds of literature they contain.

Historical Criticism builds on these literary results. It attempts to decide when books were written, how well they fit their historical context, and what the true course and meaning of events was. This last problem of meaning leads into Theological Criticism, which is concerned solely with the meaning of the teaching and witness of the Bible. It describes and compares the thought of the two Testaments and their various books, seeing how much diversity and unity there is. It attempts to answer the question: what is the essential message of the Bible?

The task of Biblical Criticism, which the next five chapters will present, is a cooperative work aiming at a common goal. The complexity of this ancient library is such that it takes a team to get God's Word clearly understood. In a similar way the news gets to us today only through the cooperation of reporter, editor, typesetter and deliveryman. No step can be eliminated without depriving us of accurate news. Likewise, no step in understanding the Bible can be eliminated without distorting God's Word to us.

WHAT IS LITERARY CRITICISM?

Literary Criticism is the attempt to understand the Bible as literature in the same way we understand other literature that we know. The assumptions, questions, and techniques that are used to understand other works of literature are used on the Bible to understand it better. This aim needs to be emphasized. Literary Criticism of Shakespeare's plays does not result in rejecting or denigrating these great monuments of the English language. Rather, it results in a knowledge of what Shakespeare originally wrote, where he got the basic stories, and what he meant to convey to his readers. Literary Criticism brings out the truth of literature; it does not refute it.

Before the coming of Biblical Criticism, the Bible was virtually placed in a glass case so that it could be admired from a distance, but studied only by a privileged few. During the Middle Ages the Church did not allow the Bible to be translated into the common languages of its people. They could not even admire it; they simply heard those parts the priests and popes relayed to them. Thus very few people really understood how it arose, where it came from and what it had to say to contemporary men. Biblical Criticism began the study of the Bible as a book needing serious consideration as literature. It needs the best of man's mind to delve into it and understand it. Answers are not easily found. Instead, man must give his best effort to find them.

Literary Archaeology

The questions that are asked by literary critics are manifold: is this document a unit in itself or is it made up of more than one original document? Who wrote it? What kind of literature is it? What is the meaning of the words and conventions used in writing it?

A variety of methods have been developed to answer these questions. The unity of a document is determined by comparing the language, background, and thought of its various parts. The authorship is sought from internal evidence of style, language and ideas, and external evidence of attestation. The kind of literature involved is found by comparing the writing with the established forms of literature (poetry, parable, sermon, etc.). The meaning of the document is decided by comparison with other writings of that language and time, whose words and conventions have already been elucidated.

This procedure has points of similarity with many of the sciences, particularly those like archaeology which are not basically experimental but seek to explain what has been given. The archaeologist develops methods for dating different levels of a dig in much the same way that a literary critic develops means of determining the author of a document. The archaeologist must learn to interpret the meaning of artifacts and buried buildings by comparing discoveries with knowledge of other digs. In a similar way the literary critic learns to interpret his artifacts, which happen to be documents. In both professions there is considerable leeway for differences of opinion, but both do develop many conclusions with which most scholars in the field agree.

The Need for a Viewpoint

The assumption behind literary study of the Bible is that in fact it is a book in some ways like other books. To a certain extent this is valid. The Old Testament is the collection of Hebrew songs, chronicles, sermons and theological treatises that remain from the period up to about 150 BC. The New Testament is a collection of the letters, sermons, histories, etc., of the earliest church, up to perhaps AD 125. The Bible is literature. But is it literature like all other literature? Is it even literature like other religious literature? That depends on what comparisons are made. Certainly, the message of the Bible is different from all other literature and cannot be measured or interpreted accurately by making it conform to what is known of other works of religious literature, any more than Shakespeare's plays can be deeply understood by lumping them together with all other drama.

But the *form* and *history* of the Bible's literature are similar enough to that of other types of literature for comparisons to be valuable. The Fundamentalist, of course, denies this. In particular, he says, all other literature has errors of fact or interpretation, but the Bible is the Word of God and so has no errors. If that position is adopted, then most literary criticism is excluded, but the majority of the Church today is not willing to take that position. Instead, it sees the Bible as a human book (as well as an inspired one) which must be studied by the methods that have become appropriate for the study of human books. By this study considerable insight will be gained, but the most profound level of the Bible — its inspired message — will be neither confirmed nor disproved. In a similar way scientific observation of man provides great insight into the human species, but man's depths — his personhood — cannot be reached by science's objective methods.

In this chapter we will not study all of the questions raised by Literary Criticism, but only a sampling of the more important of them. By doing this we shall try to see what methods are used and to decide if they are appropriate for the task of approaching the Bible. We shall see that the methods are mostly useful, but give only preliminary, not final, answers to many of our questions. In no area is this more true than in deciding what kind of literature the Bible contains.

INTERPRETATION BY CLASSIFICATION

Perhaps the most basic of all the tasks of Literary Criticism is the classification of the various types of literature, for it is only when we know what we are dealing with that we can know how best to interpret it. At one time in the Church it was thought that the Bible was largely allegory, and so scholars spent their time trying to dream up allegorical interpretations for every story and number in the Bible.

Later, after the Reformation, it was thought that there were only two basic types of literature in the Bible, literal and symbolic. Fundamentalists still make this distinction, saying that the proper method of biblical interpretation is to take everything possible as literal, and to use this for interpreting the rest which is symbolic. Of course this immediately raises the question of what can be taken as literal, but Fundamentalists seem to have fairly general agreement among themselves as to which is which.

In the last one hundred years the categories of literature found in the Bible have been seen to be far, far broader than was ever thought before. Not all the following types of literature had been previously ignored, but biblical criticism has spotlighted the most debatable types.

Sermon

One of the primary categories of the Bible is the Sermon. A sermon is essentially a second-hand report of God's revelation and intentions, delivered by one who believes God has sent him to speak. Millions of them are heard around the world every week. The first biblical sermons were given by the prophets of the Old Testament. Whenever we turn to their writings, for example to Isaiah 7, we see that the prophets brought various messages from God to man. They begin, "Thus says the Lord," and go on to proclaim the message they believe has been given to them. In the same way the New Testament is filled with sermons. The clearest examples are found in Acts (e.g. 2:14-36), where the apostles stand up and bear witness to what they have seen and heard and tell the meaning of the life, death and resurrection of Jesus.

But how far does this category extend? For example, can we speak of the chapters of the Gospel of John as sermons on the theme of the life and teachings of Jesus? There are extensive differences between the picture of Jesus in John and the picture given in the Synoptic Gospels, differences that suggest that these are two different kinds of literature, having different origins.

Perhaps the most striking differences are these: in the Gospel of John the teaching of Jesus is given in long, complex, circular discourses that usually deal with one subject; however, in the Synoptic Gospels Jesus never gives a speech like that, but He always is reported speaking in short, epigrammatic sayings, or in parables.

Secondly, the central emphasis of the teaching of the Gospel of John is Jesus' person, origin, authority, and relationship to God, whereas in the Synoptics the central emphasis is the Kingdom of God and the way of life — discipleship — to which Jesus calls those who hear Him. Could it be then that the Gospel of John does not represent a verbatim account of what Jesus taught? Is it rather a book of devotional sermons in the first person designed to explain the meaning of Jesus, and the author's understanding of His authority? These words of interpretation were given as Jesus' own because the author believed that the Risen Christ was the One who had brought this understanding. The truth of this understanding does not depend on whether these are the words of the earthly Jesus or are the inspiration that came after His resurrection.

It is certain that the Gospel of John is interpretation of the meaning of Jesus, and the truth of interpretation seldom depends on who first enunciates it. Louis XV may or may not have said, "After me, the deluge," but it was certainly an accurate interpretation of the times. John Kennedy may or may not have meant his inaugural to signify a new era of youth participation in democracy, but in fact it was that. No matter whether Jesus Himself said it or not the truth still stands — He is the Way, the Truth and the Life.

Understanding the Gospel of John as sermons and not as journalism changes our understanding of the teaching of Jesus, but in no way eliminates the Church's universal belief that these sermons give a true interpretation of the meaning of Jesus.

Poetry

A second category of the literature of the Bible is that of Poetry. It has always been recognized that there was poetry in the Bible, and that this had to be interpreted as poetry and not as rhyming or rhythmical prose. The central characteristic of poetry is its imagery which cannot be taken literally.

In the modern world we can tell what is poetry by rhymes or rhythms or poetic form, but ancient poetry did not necessarily have any of these. Thus, detection of poetry often must come by the content and meaning, not from its formal characteristics. Modern examples of this same kind of poetry are often found in song titles such as, "I am a Rock," "The Sounds of Silence," or "I am the Walrus."

Sometimes there is no problem in understanding poetry: "The Lord is my shepherd" is understood by all, even by children, to mean something different from a prose statement, "The Lord is a shepherd," which would mean that He takes care of sheep. But other lines cause trouble. When the Psalmist says, "O give thanks to the God of gods," are we to take this to mean that there are a variety of gods and the God of Israel is the chief One? Or is this simply a poetic exclamation of the sovereignty of the Lord?

Not only do we have a problem in knowing exactly how to interpret the material that all agree is poetry, we also have great difficulty in deciding what is poetry, or rather, what is poetic and symbolic and not to be taken literally. When these words are found in the mouth of God, "I repent of the evil which I did to you" (Jer. 42:10), are we to take them as literal truth, or a poetic way of speaking of God's mercy?

Jesus' teaching presents this same problem, for He often used Hebrew poetry in His teaching, leaving us with a problem in interpretation: "Whoever says, 'You fool' shall be liable to the hell of fire" (Matt. 5:22). Are we to take this to be prose and so interpret it literally? Or is it poetic exaggeration for effect, emphasizing the point that it is not only overt action against our brother that matters but also what we say and think of him?

Answers to these questions only come by comparing these sayings with the rest of His teaching and with other Jewish writings of the time, trying to determine by this means what is poetry and what is prose.

Parable

A third literary form found in the Bible is Parable. A parable is a short story with a message, usually a one-sentence message at the conclusion. Jesus' parables are illustrations of some point of His preaching, and often need interpretation. For instance, an interpretation is added in the last verse to "The Lost Sheep" (Luke 15:3ff.). Jesus also told parables that did not need interpretation, but were stories to illustrate some human way of life which He commended, like the story of the Good Samaritan (Luke 10:30ff.).

The most common modern examples of parables are probably sermon illustrations. Both of Jesus' types of parables, illustrative stories like "The Good Samaritan," and stories needing application and interpretation like "The Lost Sheep" are found in sermons.

If a preacher wishes to illustrate his point that love is stronger than hatred, he may well tell a story in which the love of one person outlasted and eventually broke through the hatred of another. That would be an illustrative story. On the other hand, he might tell how Greece was militarily conquered by Rome but then was able to infiltrate its culture into Rome and make it culturally Greek. Then the interpretation could be given, "In the same way, love, which appears weaker than hatred, will eventually conquer it." This latter type of parable, in which an interpretation must be sought, is the chief type of parable in the New Testament.

Allegory

A fourth type of literature is called Allegory. This, too, is a short story with a message, but unlike a parable its message is not contained basically in the climax. Rather, an allegory has secret meanings woven into its whole structure, with each of the characters and events described having a meaning that is known only to the initiated few.

The best examples of this type of writing are found in the book of Daniel. For example, in Daniel 7 there is a vision of four "beasts" which represent the four empires that have overcome Israel. The figure "like a son of man" stands for Israel. "Horns" represent kings. "A time, two times and half a time" probably represents three and one-half years. The story was originally told in this form so that only those who know these keys to it could understand. They would then understand the message to mean that Greece, which was then (165 BC) ruling Israel, would shortly be destroyed by God. In the text of Daniel 7, an interpretation of the allegory has been added to make its point clear.

Allegory is not a common literary form in the modern world, but it is not totally absent. A possible example is the movie, "Cool Hand Luke." Luke was a free man who became a prisoner because of his own initiative in attacking the powers that hold men prisoner. Luke becomes the center of the other prisoners' lives, giving himself to them to the extent even of suffering agony for them. He gives his mother over to the protection of another and shows his fellow prisoners the way to freedom. The imprisoning powers finally kill him but cannot quiet him because his followers spread the word of the way he was able to be free even while in prison. The movie can be seen as an allegory of the life and significance of Christ, a point that viewers recognize once they have been given the key.

There is a dispute in biblical scholarship over whether or not Jesus ever used allegory. There is no doubt that the New

Testament thought He did, for the interpretation given to the parable of The Sower (Mark 4:14ff.) presents hidden meanings for all the elements of Jesus' story. Some scholars contend that Mark's interpretation is a later addition, that in fact Jesus' original meaning was simply, "Even though a great deal of waste motion goes into the work of the Kingdom of God, still God will bring a magnificent harvest." As poetry critics often see much more in a poem than the author intended, so, it is said, the early Church saw much more in Jesus' parables than He intended.

The dispute is not yet settled. It is agreed by most scholars that the Church down through the ages was wrong in seeking allegorical meanings in most of Jesus' parables. But there is no agreement over The Sower. Another story that appears to require an allegorical interpretation is The Wicked Husbandmen (Mark 12:1ff.), which seems to demand that the following equations be made: "Vineyard" = Israel; "tenants" = leaders of Israel; "owner" = God; "Servants" = prophets; "beloved son" = Jesus; "death" = Jesus' crucifixion; "others" = Gentiles. As the story now stands, that is the way it should be interpreted. Some scholars assert that Jesus did not tell this story at all, saying that "Jesus usually did not tell allegories." That is true, but is not an adequate reason for asserting that He never did. Jewish rabbis told allegories in Jesus' day, and so it would be surprising if Jesus had not also used that form.

Short Story

A parable is a story of fiction usually of a paragraph or less. This type of literature is not limited to the teaching of Jesus, for it is found also in the Old Testament, as in Isaiah 5, where another parable of a vineyard is given. Some scholars claim that there is also an extended work of fiction in the Old Testament, which could be labelled a short story with a moral, or perhaps a novelette. This is the book of Jonah, which is unique among the prophetic books of the Old Testament in that it does not consist of prophetic oracles, but is the story of a reluctant prophet.

The reason for calling Jonah a novelette is not because of the miraculous events that happen in it. There are miraculous events throughout most of the Old Testament, and the books that they are found in are not called fiction. The reason for giving Jonah this designation is the fact that it is a work of art. It has literary unity and form: a beginning, middle, and end. It has characterization and purpose with one central point being made. It is unlike any life of a Hebrew prophet known in the Old Testament, and it conveys a message that was often rejected in Israel: that God cares about the people of other nations in just the way He cares about Israel.

It is certainly possible that this short story is based upon a historical character or incident, but the development and moral show its present form to be a work of art. Many modern works of fiction have a similar foundation upon which a literary structure is built. For example the novel, *The King Must Die* is based on an ancient Greek tradition about Theseus, King of Athens, but in its form and detail it is a work of fiction.

Myth

Another type of literature found in the Bible and somewhat related to fiction and to parable, is Myth. We shall discuss this category at considerable length in a later chapter. Here it is important to see that all scholars agree that there is some myth in the Bible. Myth is very difficult to define accurately, and indeed much debate centers on its exact definition. Basically, a myth is a poetic story about God or the gods which means to convey eternal truth in symbolic form. Myth is especially used to describe the beginning and the end of the world, events about which man has no direct knowledge. Myths in this literary sense are not simply falsehoods. Rather they are symbolic means of proclaiming truth about God that cannot as well be conveyed in abstract, purely rational, forms.

It would be generally agreed, even by Fundamentalists, that the Bible refers to Babylonian myths. When we read the following words, they must be interpreted in light of the Babylonian myth of creation: "Was it not Thou that didst cut Rahab in pieces, that didst pierce the dragon?" (Is. 51:9).

Rahab was a dragon, the goddess of Chaos whom the high god Marduk killed, and whose body was used by him as the foundation for the earth and for heaven. The Hebrews did not *believe* this myth, for their stories of creation are different, but they did *use* the myth as part of their poetic exaltation of God the Creator.

While all scholars would agree that the reference to Rahab is mythology, there is much greater debate over the Genesis stories of the beginning of the world and visions of the end in Daniel, Joel, and New Testament writings. Generally, it is agreed that there are picturesque, poetic elements in these accounts that should not be taken literally, but it is debated how much must be understood as myth.

Such an understanding does not destroy the value of the stories, but takes them out of the realm of history in which they are merely past or future and makes them present. For example, understanding the Adam stories as myth means seeing them as a description of every man's rebellion, of our rebellion today, and so not allowing us to relegate them to an era that is past and really of no pressing significance to modern man. Thus the writer of Genesis could have presented eternal truth in the form of myth.

Modern writers sometimes do this same thing. C. S. Lewis wrote a novel entitled *Till We Have Faces*, which is an allegory of the relationship between Christ and the Christian. The story, however, is based on the ancient Greek myth of Cupid and Psyche, which tells of the love of a princess for a mountain spirit. Lewis was not claiming that the myth was true, but he still used it to express the truth of the Christian's love for God.

Legend and Chronicle

Myth, which is not based on any direct historical knowledge, must be distinguished from "Legend," which is an expansion of an historical foundation by the addition of tales of great feats or miracles. Elijah and Elisha were historical characters, but a certain number of the stories surrounding them are legendary. A good example is Elijah's ascent to heaven in a chariot of fire. In our culture, also, legends grow about historical characters, like the story of George Washington throwing a silver dollar across the Potamac. The most important debate in biblical discussion of this category is whether the Patriarchal Narratives (Genesis 12-50) are legends or not. Their background details are often authentic, so the stories might be also. But the stories were written down five hundred years after the events, so legends had time to grow.

Certainly, some legendary details were added over five hundred years, so those narratives must be distinguished from "Chronicles" which are direct reports of the outward course of events. The best Old Testament example of this type of writing is "The Court Chronicle of David" (2 Sam. 9-20), which many scholars think was written by an eye-witness. A very similar type of document is Arthur Schlesinger's A *Thousand Days*, which is an insider's report of what took place in the Kennedy administration. It was written in the emotion of the moment, before time and new facts gave the possibility of a complete view. In a real sense, then, Chronicle is journalism rather than history, for interpretation and connection with later events is an essential mark of historical writing.

No journalism is completely free of interpretation, however. The Court History of David is no exception, for the author in several places expresses his faith that the events that took place were due to the work of the Lord. Likwise, Schlesinger's chronicle expresses his faith that Kennedy was an outstanding president who contributed immensely to the health of the nation. For the most part, though, both of those works were mainly concerned to report the outward course of events.

Salvation History

Most of the Bible is not intended to be journalism, but history, for the writers are greatly concerned to emphasize their interpretation of events. The biblical history is a peculiar type of history. When we read the history of the Second World War, we would be very surprised to see the interpretation that Hitler was defeated because God had created an alliance against him. But the Bible is full of such assertions. Everything of any importance that took place was understood to be the result of God's action.

This fact has led scholars to suggest that the Bible speaks about a special type of history, called "Salvation History," because it is the story of God's dealings with man for his salvation. Other scholars assert that this is not a different type of literature but is simply myth. Which of these two is correct will have to be discussed in the chapter on "Demythologizing." Clearly the crucial decision about what type of literature this is depends on a basic understanding of God and how He acts in the world.

The most important examples of "Salvation History" are found in the Gospels. These four short writings are unlike any other literature with which we are familiar. They have been called biographies. But biography, like Sandburg's *Lincoln* starts with youth and upbringing, physical characteristics and mental traits, and proceeds in an orderly and connected fashion until the end, at Ford's Theater. The Gospels omit much of that, and add many references to God and His activity in the life, death, and resurrection of their Subject. Apparently, the Gospels must be treated as a unique type. Everything in them concentrates on The Message: in this Man, God has fulfilled His promise to save His people.

Whether or not this message is true cannot be determined by literary criticism. Instead, it is a problem that must be turned over to the historian and the theologian. In a sense the literary critic is like a television reporter on a political convention floor who unearths a startling rumor. The reporter can only say that this is a unique report, unlike anything else he has heard. Then he must leave it to the "anchorman" in the central booth to determine from his broader perspective whether it is likely to be true.

These, then, are the various types of literature found in the Bible.

SONS AND COUSINS

One of the chief aims of literary criticism is to try to determine how various books are related to each other, for some books are very similar to each other, as the books of Kings and Chronicles are, and as Colossians and Ephesians are. In the modern world, questions of similarities between books are eliminated by observance of copyright laws. In newspapers, however, there is continuous cannibalism in major news stories, as reporters write about what other reporters have written, as well as what they have observed themselves. An historian trying to decipher the Bay of Pigs story would have to estimate what the relationship was between the newspaper stories, Kennedy biographer accounts, and various Cuban reports. Only by knowing which stories depend on which other stories will the true report begin to filter through.

Theories

The most important example in the Bible of closely related books are the three Synoptic Gospels which have a great deal of material in common. How do we explain the common material? The most advocated and probable conclusions were as follows.

In the early Church, when Matthew was the most popular Gospel, it was thought that Mark was a later, shortened version of Matthew. This is the official position of the Roman Catholic church today. Another popular theory has been that all three Gospels are dependent on an "oral gospel," a gospel that existed only in the oral tradition which all three of the Gospel writers received. A third theory is that Matthew is dependent upon Mark, and Luke is dependent on both of them together. None of these three theories is widely accepted by Protestant scholars today.

It is the generally agreed conclusion of biblical scholarship that Mark is the first Gospel, and that Matthew and Luke independently used Mark as the basis for their own Gospels. This solution was suggested over one hundred years ago and has since been adopted by a great many literary critics as best explaining the observable facts. That is all the solution does. It is not a provable conclusion; it simply has fewer difficulties, and explains more facts, than do the other hypotheses.

Facts

The facts that need to be explained are basically these: (1) the three Gospels have sections which are almost word-for-word the same in Greek. It is primarily this fact that eliminates the hypothesis that all three are dependent on an oral gospel. Such a gospel would probably be in Aramaic, the language Jesus spoke, and would have considerable variety in the translations used by the Evangelists. A story told to a neighbor over the backyard fence will have changed substantially by the time it has circled the neighborhood, and is unlikely to retain any large share of the original words. If the story has to be translated from one language to another as it makes its rounds, the likelihood of exact words being remembered is even less.

(2) Mark, the shortest Gospel, has stories with many more details than the other Gospels. In addition it lacks much of the teaching found in Matthew and Luke, concentrating in-

stead largely on events. It is difficult to imagine why Mark would eliminate most of the teaching in order to provide room for more unimportant details. It is this fact that virtually eliminates the suggestion that Mark is a shortened version of Matthew. Rather it seems more likely that Mark gave all the material he had, and that Matthew and Luke eliminated many of his details to make room for the extensive teaching material which they both received.

(3) Finally, a substantial portion of the teaching material found in Matthew and Luke is common to both (and not found in Mark). Matthew never places this common teaching material in the same context that Luke does. For example, they both have the Lord's Prayer, but in Luke it is placed in the Journey to Jerusalem (Luke 11), while in Matthew it is placed at the beginning of the Galilean ministry (Matthew 6). This fact eliminates the suggestion that Luke is dependent on Matthew, or vice versa: neither would be so foolish as always to remove the non-Markan material from the context the other had put it in. It is more reasonable to believe that Matthew and Luke both had another written document (named "Q") other than Mark, and that independently they combined Mark and Q. It is no wonder that they never combined them in the same way. This is what is known as the "two document hypothesis," Mark and Q being the two original documents.

Scientific Detection

This is the way literary criticism operates. It seeks out the observable facts and then tries to explain them. It is the same sort of procedure that scientists follow when they are dealing with natural phenomena. They observe what happens and then try to explain it. The difference between most sciences and literary criticism is that the literary critic cannot invent experiments by which he can test his hypothesis. The facts are there already in the Gospels. We cannot create any more facts as the scientist can by devising a new experiment.

Literary criticism is therefore unlike the experimental sciences, but similar to the descriptive sciences like Archaeology or Astronomy. It is perhaps even more closely related to a new science, Criminology. The detective is a good parallel to the literary critic when he is attempting to determine the relationships between two documents. Both must work with the facts that are given; no new experiments can be devised. But methods of detecting even the most minute and hidden facts must constantly be devised if progress is to be made.

Once all the observable evidence has been found, then the detective, literary or criminal, must put the evidence together to make a coherent pattern, a reasonable plot that explains the evidence best. Several patterns may have to be tried before an adequate one appears, and it may need refining before it is fully accepted. All this searching for evidence, creating patterns and refining them, took almost a century in the study of the Gospels. Now most scholars believe the essential solution has been found.

The "two document hypothesis" is as close to a scientific conclusion as can be reached, as is shown by the almost universal agreement of Protestant critics. The result of this century-long search is that now we know what documents are the closest to the original events. If we want accurate knowledge of Jesus' life and teaching, we must turn first to these two original sources, Mark and Q.

SEARCH FOR AN AUTHOR

Books That Grow

One of the chief tasks of Literary Criticism is deciding by whom a given piece of literature was written. This involves dating the work, and also deciding whether the book was written over a number of years (or centuries) or is a literary unity as it stands. The question of unity is answered by looking at the language, style, historical background, theological emphasis and purpose of the various parts of the work.

In the Old Testament, for example, it has come to be agreed by most scholars that the book of Isaiah was not written by one man. The first 39 chapters were to a large extent written by Isaiah, the son of Amoz, as the beginning of the book claims, but the rest of the work was added on at a later date. The most important evidence for this is the fact that Isaiah wrote to people who were in Palestine awaiting the invasion of the Assyrians, about 700 BC. Chapters 40-55 (known as Second Isaiah) were written to the Israelite exiles in Babylon who were awaiting their return to Israel about 540 BC. Besides this difference of background, there is also a substantial difference of emphasis in the theology of the two prophets.

In the twentieth century this problem arises when two men have co-authored a book. Then critics sometimes attempt to determine where one author left off and the other began.

A similar situation concerns the Pentateuch, the first five books of the Old Testament. For example, Genesis 1 and 2 seem to give two differing accounts of creation, and indeed use two different names for God (Elohim in Genesis 1 and Yahweh Elohim in Genesis 2). Literary critics have sifted the material in the Pentateuch and come up with the hypothesis that there are four basic documents here, written in stages beginning about the ninth century BC and ending about the fifth century BC. Other critics deny that we can speak of actual "documents" but only of stages of development, and there is no complete agreement about those stages.

The debate is still wide open and the results are not yet in, except for the agreed conclusion that the Pentateuch was written over a period of centuries by a number of different authors and editors. A comparable conclusion may arise when the United States is dust and a civilization three thousand years from now tries to determine who was the author of our Constitution.

Elusive Authors

In the New Testament similar discussions have taken place concerning authorship. None of the Gospels makes any mention of its author, so there has been considerable debate over them. The debate centers on the question whether or not the traditions of the Church in the second and third centuries are right in naming our Gospels. The arguments are complex and indecisive, for the evidence is inadequate to supply definite conclusions.

In modern literature there is usually no problem in determining authorship because writers usually attach their names to their documents. Occasionally anonymous works appear, such as the celebrated article in *Foreign Affairs* magazine in 1947 that first presented the concept of "containment" of Communism. It was signed by a mysterious "X." It was immediately surmised that the author was a State Department officer whose concept was not official policy. This guess was eventually confirmed as truth when George Kennan, later a United States Ambassador to Russia and Yugoslavia, acknowledged it as his. In the Bible, however, the authors are long dead and give no such help.

Still there is considerable evidence about the authorship of some of the disputed works of the New Testament, in particular, evidence that they were *not* written by their traditionally named authors. Hebrews was said by some in the early Church to have been written by Paul, but the letter does not claim this (as all Paul's letters do), and the style and content are so different from Paul's authentic letters that there is probably no scholar today who would claim it as Pauline. The Second Epistle of Peter is so different from the First Epistle that they cannot be by the same author (who may or may not be the Apostle Peter). Many arguments are used to demonstrate this, but in this case the differences of language are decisive, for the two books have only about one-third of their words in common.

It is virtually impossible for one man to write two letters and not use approximately 75 percent of the same words.

The Limitations of Computers

Counting words is not an absolutely decisive method of guaging authorship, however, because it is not completely clear how much similarity there should be between various works. For example, one quarter of the words used in Romans are not found in Paul's other letters and no one questions his authorship of this letter. Yet his authorship of Ephesians and the Pastorals (I and II Timothy, Titus) is questioned on these grounds: about one-third of the words of the Pastorals are different from the other Paulines, and some say this is too many. Ephesians has only one-sixth of its words different from other Paulines, so it is said this is too few, that Ephesians must have been virtually copied from Colossians which it resembles closely. There is no general agreement over these two questions, though there is more agreement that the Pastorals are not Pauline, than that Ephesians is not (for could not Paul himself have done the copying?).

The most important words to be observed are the less significant ones, the "rathers," "therefores," and "buts," for they are the most characteristic marks of an author's style. Nouns and verbs are mainly dependent on subject matter and so vary from letter to letter, but other words remain virtually the same for all letters a man writes. The same kinds of clues are sought in modern literary detection, especially in the analysis of handwriting. A man may change many of the most obvious marks of his writing, but an expert will be able to detect dozens of minute characteristics that cannot be successfully disguised.

Theological differences are considered also, but there is much wider dispute over that criterion, because what one scholar calls a difference, another scholar calls a development of thought. How much variation are we likely to find in the thought of one author? That is a question to which there is no conclusive answer. It would be clear, though, that if two letters had nothing in common, and much contradiction, they could not be by the same author, no matter whether the same man's name was attached to them or not. It was by this criterion that many scholars in the early Church came to the conclusion that the Gospel of John and Revelation could not have been written by the same John.

CONCLUSION

This stroll through the groves of Literary Criticism has brought into the open a number of interesting insights. While this discipline cannot solve all the problems that are raised, still in some cases it can produce fairly certain conclusions concerning the growth of books, or the evidences of authorship. Other results are debatable, such as the authorship of the Gospels and what books or passages fall into the categories of poetry, allegory, myth, novelette, etc. In these cases Literary Criticism is not a science, but an art.

As with all arts, the participation of the viewer or reader is required. This means that literary study of the Bible, far from relieving Christians of the task of reading the Bible, should by its nature strongly encourage them to read and reread it, more intelligently every time. Literary scholarship supplies many useful facts and suggestions, but it cannot finally determine the meaning for us today. That is a challenge that is left to the reader who can be helped in this task by the disciplines of historical and theological criticism, which we shall now investigate.

6

God's History Book

The Bible is a book of history. It was written in particular historical periods and is a product of those times. Therefore, if it is to be properly understood, it must be seen against the background of the days of its birth. In addition it deals with historical events, pointing to particular episodes of the past and saying that they are of central importance to all men. These important happenings make up the story of God's people, from their beginnings to the formation of the Church. Not only does the Bible present the outward course of events, but like any good history book it strives to give the meaning of what happened; it presents interpretation of what occurred — causes and effects, historical significance, and eternal importance. Understanding and interpreting books of history is the work of Historical Criticism. In order to understand how Historical Criticism aids in the interpretation of the Bible, it is necessary to know what history is and how historians usually work.

The Problem Of History

THE REPORTER AT WORK

History is not one thing but two: it is the substance of the past — the event that took place — and it is also the report of the past. The historian's job is to create the report so that it will be as accurate a mirror of the events as possible. He does this by seeking out people, papers, and pottery. If at all possible, he wants eyewitnesses to tell him what they remember. He also wants to read all the existing written reports. Supplementing both of these is the evidence of artifacts — coins, pottery, buildings, gravestone inscriptions, and other interesting phenomena that testify to past events.

In principle, writing history is like reporting news. The reporter is interested in writing a story to reflect the events. He seeks out the participants, if any are available, to get their story, but he does not stop there. He reads any relevant documents, police reports, coroner's reports, or other newspaper reports, until he has as full a written account as he can find. He then goes to the scene of the events in order to see what evidence can be gleaned from the lay of the land, fragments lying about or any other physical reminders.

Once he has collected all his evidence, the historian must decide what to write. He must always be selective because he does not have space to include all the evidence he has collected. He must always offer an interpretation of what happened because the evidence never speaks completely for itself. Simply by selecting what he considers to be relevant evidence, the historian interprets, offering his own understanding of what happened.

SCIENCE OR ART

In one sense writing history is like doing research in natural science: both scientist and historian must collect all the evidence that is available and then weave it together to create a pattern that makes sense. Unlike the scientist, however, the historian cannot run experiments. He cannot create new facts by repeated observations. He cannot test his conclusions by new experiments. This means that the historian must be more of an artist than the scientist. He must depend more on imaginative insight because he does not have the great accumulation of facts or resources for testing that the scientist has.

The second difference between a scientist and an historian is that the scientist is a detached, objective observer at all times, but the historian must be sympathetically involved in his subject if he is to understand it fully. The scientist cannot feel what it is like to be an atom. The historian can "enter into" the situation of Jesus' disciples in Jerusalem after Jesus' death and so better understand them. Naturally, this procedure will allow differing interpretations because different historians sympathize differently, but still it must be done if the deepest meaning of events is to be found.

THE ROLE OF ASSUMPTIONS

As in all intellectual activity, the historian, too, operates by assumptions. He assumes that basic logic must not be contravened — that two and two do not equal five, and that one man cannot be in two places at the same time. He also assumes that the test of truth is the sufficiency and coherence of evidence. Only when the evidence is sufficient and fits together adequately can he conclude that he has reached the truth. Naturally there will be varying degrees of confidence depending upon the evidence. When parents come home and find their living room in a shambles, they will not conclude they know exactly what happened until they have reports from all involved and have been able to fit the reports together with the visible evidence to create a coherent account.

One factor that will enter into the parents' determination of what happened is their prior assumption of the way things usually happen around their house. Likewise, the historian must operate with assumptions about the way things happen in the universe. Some historians used to assume that history operated as Darwin understood biology — that progress was the nature of history. Others assume that nothing takes place that cannot be explained by presently known natural laws. The

Christian assumes from his experience that God is active in history and cannot be neglected if a true understanding, especially of Israel and the Church, is to be found. All historians write on the basis of their personal philosophies, none of which can be proved or disproved. Especially, when studying the Bible, this insight is important, for it means that we need not be agnostics in order to be historians.

This does not mean that we are to be indiscriminantly subjective in deciding on the best assumptions to be held in approaching the Bible. Some presuppositions held by Christians are better than others, as the discussion of Fundamentalism attempted to show. Deciding on the proper viewpoint for approaching the Bible is perhaps the most difficult task a reader has to face. He must strive to combine the Bible's own understanding of reality, which is disputed, with whatever is necessary for modern thinking, which is also disputed. But continual discussion, such as this book presents, will help individual Christians decide for themselves what assumptions they feel required to adopt in trying to understand the Bible.

HISTORICAL PROBLEMS

Many historical problems confront the reader of the Bible. But if there is one central question that has agitated historical critics for the last century, it is the question of the origin of Christianity. The New Testament says that the origin of the Church was in the life, teaching, death, and resurrection of Jesus, but some critics have claimed that this was a later theory imposed upon the facts. In a similar manner, critics of the Warren Commission say that its report, which says only Oswald shot President Kennedy, is a theory that hides the truth.

Was the origin of Christianity, in fact, to be found, as Marx believed, somewhere in the second century, among preachers who invented the story of Jesus and wrote mythical stories about Him as other gods have myths written about them? Or was classical Liberalism right in saying that Paul was really the originator, the one who took the simple ethical teachings of a Jewish rabbi and transformed them into a Greek religion of redemption? Or is *The Passover Plot*, a recent novel, correct in asserting the origin really is found in the first disciples who mistakenly (or perhaps maliciously) claimed that He had risen from the dead? The answer to this question can only come by digging deeply into the documents of the New Testament and the early Church. Let us look at some typical problems that illustrate the assumptions and methods used.

The problems to be dealt with here are those that are common to every historical task. In the first place the *Authenticity* of the documents must be validated. If we wish to know about something in the past we must take the reports and ask, "Are they truly what they claim to be? Do they offer reliable evidence of the events they report?"

Next, what is the *Relationship* between the reports being studied and other evidence of the period? Does outside evidence provide information on the existence, dating, and meaning of the characters or events reported? Are there conflicts between the reports we are studying and background material from the period, or does the background confirm the biblical material?

Then the particular *Events* of the documents before us must be studied closely. We must ask several questions: How extensive is the evidence for any particular event, say the ressurection of Jesus? Does the evidence fit together, or are there contradictions? What seems possible and likely?

Finally, connected with determining what happened, we must seek the *Interpretation* of the events. We are interested not only in what happened, but also in what caused it, what significance it had, what happened as a result of it? The historian is more interested in the invisible string that makes a necklace than in the obvious stones that command our usual attention.

AUTHENTICITY

If any of the three modern theories of the origin of Christianity given in the previous section are true, then the Gospels cannot be what they appear to be. They appear to be reports of the life and teaching of Jesus. If they are fairly accurate reports, they can be called authentic.

For authenticity to be established it must be shown that they were written at a time when accurate knowledge of Jesus was available and written by someone who had access to such information. Since it is the basis for Matthew and Luke, Mark is the Gospel that is the key to the secret of the origin of Christianity.

Author, Author

It is not certain who wrote the Gospel according to St. Mark, for the Gospel itself does not say. Like the other Gospels, it received its title in the second century, reflecting the understanding of the Church at that time. It was believed that a man named Mark, a companion of the Apostle Peter, wrote the Gospel using material he had learned from Peter. No other candidate has ever been suggested as the author. Internal evidence of many stories concerning Peter adds weight to this tradition that the Gospel was written by someone who knew him. This assertion is plausible enough to command the agreement of a great many scholars.

Trying to determine who wrote an ancient book is very much like trying to determine who wrote an essay for *Time* magazine. Language, style, and content indicate only that it was one of the staff writers.

The Gospels are like *Time* articles also in that they are both composite, not the work of a single man. If Mark was the author, this means he was first a collector and editor and only secondarily an author.

The Sound of Silence

The dating of Mark's Gospel is much more an agreed conclusion than its authorship. Ancient tradition, confirmed by modern scholarship, says that the Gospel was written about the time of Peter's death, AD 64. In the ancient Jewish world knowledge was mostly carried by memory, not writing, so the need for a written tradition arose only when the apostles' memories were being silenced by death in the 60's of the first century.

An even more important factor in the dating of Mark is that it shows no knowledge of the destruction of Jerusalem in AD 70. Had Mark known about the end of the Temple, he would certainly have reflected this in the Gospel, because it was seen by the Church as a confirmation of the truth of Jesus' preaching. Likewise, if Arthur Schlesinger had known about the long, deadly, destructive Vietnamese War when he wrote about Kennedy, it would surely have been reflected in *A Thousand Days*. Lack of knowledge of our great involvement in Vietnam shows that the book was written prior to the great United States buildup and agony. By this reasoning a scholar in years to come would be able to conclude that Schlesinger wrote in the 1963-65 period. Similarly, scholars have concluded that the Gospel of Mark was written in the period AD 60-70.

Bones and Flesh

In our search into the past we as historians have concluded that the Second Gospel was written within a generation of the events it records, and within a few years at least of the death of Peter, the chief witness to those events. But how accurate are the outline and details, the bones and flesh of the Gospel?

Since many sections of the Gospel were handed down in oral tradition before they reached Mark, the more easily re-

membered forms are the most likely to be accurate. The Parables are easily remembered and so are probably close to the
words of Jesus Himself. The Miracle Stories, which abound in
Mark, also have a memorable form, so these too probably go
back to the early tradition of the life of Jesus. This does not
mean that all parables and all miracle stories are accepted as
historical. It does mean that the abundance of these stories
makes it very likely that many of them are basically accurate.
Criticism must still deal with each story individually, but we
are close to Jesus in these two types of stories. Similarly we are
close to Socrates in Plato's Dialogues when we hear Socrates
challenging the pretentious knowledge of a supposed sophisti-
cate, for Socrates was especially famous for that role.

The third type of material that is particularly close to the
life of Jesus is the story of the Passion. Unlike the rest of the
Gospel of Mark which consists of isolated units of tradition (a
story here, a saying or parable there, with no real story or geo-
graphical connection made), the Passion Story is a whole. It
has a story line, a time scale, a series of events that fit together,
and a motive for existence. It is generally agreed that the Passion Story was put together not long after Jesus' death and
resurrection as a means of proclaiming that He was not a criminal. Once again, this does not mean that all of the details of
the story are equally likely, but it does mean that the story
probably goes back to the decade after Jesus death.

Many scholars conclude that parables and miracle stories
are the most reliable material in Mark, but that the outline of
the Gospel, except for the Passion Story, is probably the author's creation. Mark wrote in much the same way Barbara
Tuchman did in *The Guns of August*. Instead of giving a
chronological account of the years before August 1914, in Part
I, she gave a topical survey of each of the great nations' plans
and condition on the eve of the conflict. The outline was thus
completely her own creation.

The examples presented in the last few pages demonstrate

the way an historical critic operates, whether he is dealing with the Bible or with any other historical document. We saw in the last chapter that Mark was probably the earliest Gospel, so that is the one we concentrate on for historical information. Then we asked who wrote it, and the answer comes back that it was probably written by a man named Mark, who probably had a close connection with Peter the Apostle, who was thereby to some degree a source for the Gospel. The Gospel was written about AD 67 as both internal and external evidence indicate. It contains some material that appears to be considerably older than its writing, that probably goes back to the witnesses to the life and teaching of Jesus. On details and the outline and the theological emphases, the critic must still continue to sift. Basically, however, historical critics believe that they can stand with confidence upon the Gospel of Mark as the most important and trustworthy witness to the life and teaching of Jesus of Nazareth that now exists.

RELATIONSHIPS

Obscurity

The second question that the historical critic must consider is how well this central witness fits the other historical evidence known from that time. For example, it must be asked whether there are any non-Christian witnesses to the death of Jesus or to His resurrection. The answer is, there are none. In fact, there are no contemporary non-Christian witnesses to the fact of His life, for He was of no importance to those who knew Him but did not believe in Him. The first clear non-Christian evidence of the existence of the Christian church comes about AD 100. All the evidence prior to that is Christian, most of it in the New Testament.

Thus, there is almost no evidence outside the New Testament that can determine the accuracy of reporting of the events of the New Testament. Some later evidence has been introduced into the discussion, for example, second century information on Jewish rules for trials before the Sanhedrin. Although these rules were not written down until about AD 200, they were in force before then, but it is not known whether they were old enough to have been in force at the time of Jesus' trial. Thus, the external evidence of the events reported in the New Testament is as meager as the chicken in a can of chicken broth.

Light

While the non-Christian writings of Jesus' day provide no real help for deciding whether or not a New Testament event took place, they do provide a great deal of help in understanding the theological meaning of New Testament writings. The main thrust of historical scholarship in its survey of non-Christian sources is the attempt to arrive at the historical sense of the New Testament, the meaning that words, phrases, and concepts had for readers of that period. In a similar way, a historian of the twenty-fifth century looking back at our period will be unable to make sense of political rhetoric unless he first understands that the word "democracy" has two entirely different meanings when used by a Communist or a Westerner.

The most important sources for understanding the New Testament are the Jewish books written in the two centuries before Christ and known as apocalyptic writings. They are given this name because they contain revelations (apocalypse = revelation) of what is to happen at the End of the World. The Dead Sea Scrolls are a very important example of that kind of literature. The Scrolls have had a substantial effect on the historical understanding of the New Testament. Probably the most important conclusion they have forced on historians is that dualistic motifs in the New Testament do not necessarily imply Greek influence. The Gospel of John presents a dualism of light and darkness, and Paul contrasted spirit and flesh. In the last century these dualisms were taken as examples of Greek corruption of the "simple gospel of Jesus," but now it is clear that Jesus could have known and used them Himself, for the Scrolls show that they are certainly Jewish and Palestinian. The Scrolls are thus a "missing link" between Judaism and the New Testament.

The Jews down through the centuries have looked upon the apocalyptic literature as heretical writings. Orthodoxy for them was symbolized by the writings of the Rabbis from AD 100-700. Until the last one hundred years Christian historians used only the "orthodox" writings as examples of Jewish thought in Jesus' time. But it became evident around 1900 that the New Testament is far closer in spirit to apocalypticism. The terms, "Kingdom of God," "Son of Man," "End of the World," have finally become clear in this century because historians discovered that the so-called "heretical" writings represented what the common people in Jesus' time believed. This type of breakthrough may happen again in centuries to come when historians studying Russia realize that official newspapers and books represent only the party line, while heretical writings like *Dr. Zhivago* represent the mind and spirit of the Russian people. The "official" story has been as whitewashed as Tom Sawyer's fence.

EVENTS

No outside literature presents any first-hand account of any event in the life of Jesus. The only sources of information extant are the writings of the New Testament. Thus, historical criticism must deal mainly with those writings, particularly the Gospels, to see whether their evidence of events is convincing.

Hidden Clues

The first things a historian seeks are contradictions between various accounts. For example, the first three Gospels say that Jesus' cleansing of the Temple took place at the end of His career, just before His death. But the Gospel of John says that Jesus visited Jerusalem more than once, and that He cleansed the Temple at the beginning, rather than at the end of His ministry. Not many historians would argue that the event happened twice. Rather, a choice must be made. In general, it seems to be probable that John is right in saying that Jesus went to Jerusalem more than once, and may be right in saying the cleansing of the Temple occurred early. The Synoptics put the cleansing at the end because they know of only one visit He made during His ministry, and that was at the end. On the other hand, it is possible that the Gospel of John was composed topically or theologically and took no account of actual chronology.

There is substantial value in contradictions for determining what happened. Contradictions provide a three-dimensional view of the event in the same way a 3-D slide viewer provides different slides for each eye.

Besides contradictions, a second type of evidence that is sought is various references to a particular type of activity or content of speech. For example, it seems clear that Jesus performed healings: because of the stories told about them, from the sayings of Jesus referring to them, and from the traditions found in Acts and the Epistles. The accumulated evidence for this is too overwhelming to discount completely. A century ago all the stories of healings were simply removed by many historians as later additions. It is now seen that they are as early in the gospel tradition as any other part, and that they are as essential to the message of the Gospel as any other part. No longer is it thought that there has to be a dichotomy: either you believe that God breaks natural law by doing miracles, *or* you must eliminate all miracle stories. The healings probably happened. That is the only way to explain the reputation Jesus received.

Extraordinary personal traits or activities thus are confirmed by the great number of references to them. For example, a recent president was reported to have appointed a man to a government post and then cancelled the appointment because the news had leaked out before he wanted it to. Such a report seems absurd, for it is hard to imagine anyone acting for such a petty motive. But similar stories about numerous other appointments have emerged so that an observer is persuaded that there must be a certain basis in truth to the accounts.

Independent Witnesses

The one event that is reported more than once in the New Testament is the resurrection of Jesus. It is the only event of any kind to which there are independent witnesses. Actually, there were no witnesses to the resurrection itself, for that supposedly took place within the cave that was used for a grave. There are not even any who claimed to be witnesses to His movement out of the grave. What is claimed is that He was dead on Friday, but on Sunday many people saw Him alive again.

The earliest evidence is given by Paul about AD 60 (I Cor. 15:5-8). There he presents the early Church's testimony which he received when he became a Christian, probably about AD 35, within five years or so of the resurrection. Paul indicates that the apostles' testimony was that Christ was seen alive after His resurrection by Peter, then by five hundred Christians (most of whom were still alive when Paul wrote and so could be asked), then by James, then by all the apostles, and then a few years later, by Paul in his conversion experience. The Gospel of Mark, written just a little later, simply proclaims the resurrection. It does not present any appearance stories, though it is possible that the end of the Gospel has been lost.

Matthew (writing about AD 80) reports that Mary Magdalene "and the other Mary" saw Him first, but that later the eleven disciples saw Him on a mountain in Galilee. Luke reports (about AD 80 also) that two apostles saw Him first, on the road to Emmaus, but that later He appeared to the eleven in Jerusalem. John reports (at an unknown date) that He was first seen by Mary Magdalene, then by all the disciples except Thomas, then by all the disciples including Thomas, then finally by seven of the leading disciples who were fishing in Galilee. The only one of these appearances that is also reported by Paul is the appearance to all the apostles, which is common to all five accounts.

No coherent story can be written by stringing these stories together. It is not that they contradict each other, but that they are completely independent of each other. By way of contrast, the Passion Story is an agreed story. All four Gospels present the same account, an account that was handed down in an oral form from the apostles. There was one story of the passion because there was probably one "official" account. For the resurrection there was no official account, for personal witness was all that had value. In Acts it can be seen that the apostles just stood up and proclaimed the resurrection, saying, "Of this we are witnesses." Everywhere they went the individuals who had seen the resurrected Jesus simply told what they had seen. No single account was ever put together because none was needed. When the time came for Paul to receive the account, for Matthew, Luke, and John to write, they merely reported the variety of accounts that they had received.

A variety of accounts by eyewitnesses was the way news travelled before the advent of the printing press. Even today, when a great event is reported, the most important evidence comes from a wide variety of people who tell what they saw. The Allied victory in World War II is very differently described by Winston Churchill, Douglas MacArthur, and Ernie Pyle, the newsman who spent the war in the trenches with the

G.I.'s. The three do not often contradict each other, but their emphasis on what was the most vital aspect of the war differed greatly. So also the resurrection accounts are the testimony of eyewitnesses who had not coordinated their stories with others, because "I was there" was the basis for their authority.

Faith and Truth

The New Testament is filled with affirmations that Jesus had been raised from the dead. Every book in the New Testament depends on that belief, for the foundation conviction of the early Church was that if there had been no resurrection there would have been no Church. Paul, initially a skeptic but then a believer within five to ten years of Easter, proclaimed that if there had been no resurrection then the whole of his gospel was worthless: "You are still in your sins" (I Cor. 15:17). He surely investigated the whole subject thoroughly. The original apostles had run away at Jesus' arrest, afraid for their own lives, but a short time later they appeared again unafraid, saying that the difference was that "God had raised Jesus from the dead."

The change in the disciples was like the change that came over Stonewall Jackson's troopers when he fought with them. When he had to stay in the background at headquarters, they were no different from any other troopers in the Confederate Army. But when he was with them in the lines, they knew no fear, fought like tigers, and were undefeated.

There is considerable evidence to attest to the truth of the disciples' witness, but it clearly is not sufficient to convince an opponent. Paul was an observer who persecuted the Church. He must have heard the apostles' testimony, but he did not believe until he himself saw the risen Christ. No one ever saw Him after death except those who believed in Him. There was no independent, unbiased, uninterested observer. The question must therefore be raised whether the testimony of believers is adequate. The problem is one of knowing whether Christians have special insight here, or are misled by a bias. If they have special insight, they are like psychoanalysts whose own experience of analysis gave them insight into its value. If Christians are simply biased, they are like anti-Semites who believe their creed because it makes them feel better.

It seems to be clear that the early Church, including the apostles who had known Him during His lifetime, believed that they had seen Him alive again after His death. It is very likely, but more disputable, that they believed the grave to have been empty on Easter Sunday morning. There are accounts of the empty grave being found. But even more important, the Jews did not believe in the immortality of the soul. Resurrection for them meant the body was raised. It is likely, therefore, that the disciples first checked the grave and were convinced there was no body there. For these reasons most observers would probably agree that the apostles thought they had seen Jesus alive after His death, believed that the grave was empty, and so concluded that He had been raised from the dead.

The beliefs and conclusion of the disciples are as far as the historian can go in describing what happened without basing any further statements on his own personal understanding of the world and God. The question that glares in the historian's face is: were the disciples right in concluding that Jesus had been raised? The debate has raged for centuries, with a variety of conclusions and explanations being presented. The historian by himself is not fully qualified to answer this question, for here theologians and philosophers must enter the discussion and debate the matter.

Enter Theology

There is no doubt that there have been in the past and continue to be today, many historians who say that "resurrections are impossible," or less bluntly, "resurrections are so unlikely that any other explanation is to be preferred." A number of such explanations are then offered to take the place of the testimony of the apostles: Jesus wasn't really dead, He had only fainted and then revived in the coolness of the grave; the disciples really didn't see Him alive, they had a collective vision which was then the source of all the other stories; they didn't really even have a vision, they just came to believe that the "spirit of Jesus" was still with them, and they described this by saying, "He is risen," and telling stories of appearances. Many other explanations have been created to explain what happened, but all of them have to deny the central evidence of the New Testament in order to stand. In a similar way different explanations of Germany's defeat in World War I were created by Hitler and others. These people found it too threatening to their nationalistic pride to admit what all the evidence exposed — Germany's army was not strong enough.

Most people decide what they think of this evidence on the basis of their philosophical and theological beliefs. If they believe that the world is governed by natural law, and that nothing happens which is not now explicable by present-day science, they will say that the resurrection could not have occurred, and some other explanation will be sought. If they believe that God is not active in the world in such a way that extraordinary events happen, then they will deny the message of the New Testament, "God has raised Him from the dead." If they believe that resurrections are so unlikely that only seeing the man dead and then alive again would be convincing, then they will never be convinced by other witnesses.

It is impossible to say precisely where we get our beliefs by which we judge such a question. But we have these beliefs, and we usually are not willing to question them. The evidence of the New Testament, however, calls us to just such a questioning. For we are confronted by the most revolutionary message anyone has ever proclaimed, "He is risen."

INTERPRETATION

The final question that the historian must ask is, "What do these events mean?" Supposing that it has been agreed that Mark is a fairly reliable witness, that the report he presents is corroborated to a certain extent by other evidence, and that the internal evidence seems sufficient to warrant the conclusion that Jesus was dead and then seen alive again. Is this important? Lazarus was dead and then seen alive again according to the Gospel of John, but no great issue was made of that. Is the resurrection simply a wonder, a miracle, something unique, like other events in the history of mankind?

Theological Conclusions

Here is where the New Testament makes its greatest point. It is not interested in the resurrection merely as an event in history. Rather it proclaims that this is *The Event*, the turning point in history by which all other events must be measured. The chain of thought of the New Testament goes something like this: (1) He was dead; (2) we saw Him alive afterwards; (3) therefore God must have raised Him from the dead; (4) therefore God has vindicated Him, and shown that Christ was His messenger who is to be believed and followed; (5) therefore His death was not for His own sins but for ours; (6) His resurrection therefore means that He is living for us now, as He died for us on the cross.

This is how the apostles interpreted the resurrection. None of it is necessary, in the sense of forcing itself upon us. Not even the conclusion that "God has raised Him" is necessary, for there may be other means of resurrection that we do not know about. The conclusions depend on the Old Testament, Jesus' teaching, and the apostles' continuing experience of the presence of Jesus in their midst. If we find ourselves within the circle of those who believe the teaching of Jesus and experience His continuing presence, then we will probably accept some of the apostles' interpretation of the resurrection. If we are not Christians, we will find ourselves rejecting that interpretation. Likewise, if we are avid Democrats, we will find ourselves looking at problems and understanding the world as Democrats do, even when we have no personal knowledge of the particular problem.

The significance of Jesus cannot be avoided by the historian, even if he rejects the Christian interpretation. The historian is called upon to explain the origin and molding forces in the lives of historic figures, and so some understanding of the resurrection faith of the disciples must be presented by even the most agnostic historian. An historian writing about Franklin D. Roosevelt must explain his popularity and appeal even if the traditional liberal picture of the "savior of his people" is rejected. The theological conclusions of the New Testament are "interpretive history" and can only be opposed by offering better interpretations.

Historical Consequences

Some historians avoid the debate on the theological significance of Jesus and the origin of the resurrection faith. They concentrate instead on the less debatable issues of what followed as a result of that faith. They ask: what was the historical consequence of the resurrection, or of the belief in the resurrection (which are identical from the historian's standpoint)? First, it gave the apostles a message for which they were willing to die. They traveled the whole of the ancient world proclaiming their amazing message, not worrying about what would happen to themselves. To a great extent, their conviction was the reason for the success of the Church's mission of planting the gospel and churches throughout the known world. One of the best parallels to that enterprise is the modern Communist International of the 1920's and 30's. Men and women believed "we have seen the future (in Russia), and it works" and so spent their lives spreading their good news.

Jesus' appearances to His first disciples were vital in their influence on Paul, the chief apostle to the Gentiles, according to the New Testament. The disciples believed that Christ had risen, and continued to proclaim this message to their fellow Jews. Only by so doing did they attract the attention of the young man Saul, who then tried to exterminate the Church. Historically speaking, it was because of his fanatical interest in the Church and its message that he came to the point where he could be converted and become the Apostle Paul. His vision on the Damascus road, in which he believed he saw and heard Jesus, depended somewhat on the stories that the Christians had already told him of Jesus' resurrection. The mission of Paul to the Gentiles depended on the resurrection faith; indeed that was the heart of his message. If there had been no resurrection faith, he would never have been a Christian or an apostle, because that decided for him between his native Judaism and the gospel to which he had been converted.

The great significance of this one event and the faith that arose from it is similar to the history of civil rights in mid-twentieth century United States of America. One event — the Supreme Court decision declaring segregated schooling illegal — was the fountain from which flowed the decisive events of the following generation. That decision created a new faith for the black man, a faith that all men should and eventually would be treated equally. That faith inspired Martin Luther King, who began the procedure of passive opposition to segregation laws and eventually caused their repeal. Like Paul, he preached his faith for all to hear, won millions of followers, and gave his life for the cause.

The early Church's resurrection belief sparked many other consequences. Enough has been said here to show why biblical historians today generally agree that the origin of the

Church is to be found in the belief of the disciples that Jesus had been raised from the dead. The evidence is sufficient for even non-Christian historians to agree that the disciples thought He had been raised. The evidence is also sufficient to show that this belief was at the center of their faith and was the motive force behind their fearless proclamation of the gospel. Historians differ on the ultimate question: What was the source of the disciples' belief in Jesus' resurrection and their belief that this implied the whole message they preached? Christians believe that God was the source. Non-Christians believe that it all came from the disciples' imagination. We must decide for ourselves.

CONCLUSION

This chapter has shown some of the issues, methods, and results of historical criticism of the Bible. How this type of study will affect Christians depends greatly on where they start. If they start with the belief that the Bible is inerrant, then historical study will be immensely disturbing, for it shows that there are contradictions, errors in detail, and challenges to the basic events of the New Testament.

If, on the other hand, a man started this study with complete skepticism about the historical value of the Bible, then he would be shaken in his skepticism and would find it difficult to deny that the Gospel of Mark is a substantially trustworthy witness to the life and teaching of Jesus. Historical study makes clear that there was no second century origin to the Christian faith, and that Paul did not corrupt a simple gospel that he received. Rather, it is practically certain that the origin of the Christian Church is found in the resurrection faith of the first disciples.

That is as far as historical study can go. The most rigorous historical scrutiny can neither affirm nor deny the central tenets of the Christian faith.

Historical criticism can say that Jesus was born about 8 BC, but it cannot say whether or not He was the Incarnate Son of God. It can say that the disciples believed He was raised from the dead, but it cannot say whether God raised Him so that His death was for our sins. It can say that the disciples' belief was the historical cause of the birth of the Christian Church, but it cannot say whether the risen Christ was the power within the Church. All of these are theological questions that cannot be answered by the historian. They will have to be taken up in the theological discussion of the last section of this study.

7

The History of God's Acts

The Bible is not a theology textbook, a set of clear-cut, unalterable doctrines that answer all man's important questions. It is, however, the fundamental source of all Christian theology, for it is a witness to man's experience of God's presence.

Unfortunately, it has taken twenty centuries for this distinction to be clearly seen. In reaction to orthodox use of the Bible as a textbook of doctrines that had to be accepted in a literal manner, scholars in the nineteenth century ignored its theological aspect as they delved into its literature and history. This one-sidedness in biblical studies resembled the narrow vision of Marxist historians who asserted that history must always be understood as the result of economic forces, basically neglecting the effects of individuals, of thought and of human aspirations.

In the late nineteenth century, scholars viewed the Bible almost exclusively as literature and history. The central result of Old Testament studies was "the history of the development of the religion of Israel from its primitive beginnings to the ethical monotheism of the prophets." In New Testament study the goal sought was a "history of the development of primitive Christianity from the simple Jewish faith of Jesus to the theology of John and Paul."

The Rebirth of Biblical Theology

A reaction developed in this century against such an exclusively historical understanding of the Bible. Scholars who were also ministers of the Church began to realize that their writings on the history of religion were irrelevant to the Church's task in the world. They began to ask themselves how they could be true to their scholarly tasks as well as to their calling as ministers of the gospel, as the economist must continually ask himself whether his ingenious theories really are of any practical value.

At the same time there was a reaction against the assumption that the Bible was primarily literature and history. It began to be seen that the Bible is not primarily interested in giving answers to historical questions, nor is it concerned to provide fascinating reading for those enthralled by ancient literature. The Bible's main concern, it came to be realized, is theology. It began to be asked whether scholars were imposing their own viewpoint on the Bible when they sought to use it mainly as an historical source. Do we correctly understand any book if we ignore its main intentions? Is *Moby Dick* really understood if it is approached as a handbook on whaling?

Allied to these two developments was a new scholarly understanding of the Bible's evidence. Scholars gradually came to see that the idea of inevitable evolutionary progress had been foisted on the biblical record. Many philosophers and historians took up Darwin's concept of progress, which made sense in biology, and used it to explain history, where it made less sense. Thus the Old Testament was used as a handbook of antiquity in which one sought materials to lay out in a line of progress. Any traits resembling those of primitive religion in other cultures were said to belong to the beginnings of Israel's faith in the time of Moses. Then this primitive faith was said to have developed into the more progressive ethical monotheism proclaimed by the prophets. So connecting steps were devised, using evidence from the Bible to show that this indeed was what happened to Israel.

The First World War brought an abrupt end to the theory of inevitable progress in history. Now we know that civilizations grow and decline and do not exhibit uniform steps along the way. It was inevitable that we would progress beyond that theory.

The synthesis of these developments was found in Karl Barth, a Swiss pastor during the First World War. He wrote a commentary on Romans which rocked the theological world in 1919, for it treated the Epistle differently than it had been treated for generations. The most recent commentaries had almost invariably tried to see where Paul's thought fit into the Jewish and Gentile religions of his day. They sought to explain where he got his theology and how it had developed from the simple Jewish faith of Jesus. Barth, however, heard God speaking to him, to the twentieth century, in the Epistle. He took Romans as a message from God that was applicable to man's situation in the crisis period of post-war Europe, rather than simply as a piece of ancient literature. And people in reading this commentary heard God speak through Romans once again, so that Karl Barth became the voice of the modern revolution in theological thinking. With the publication of Barth's *Romans* in 1919 biblical theology was reborn, as the Bible itself was reborn as the Church's authority when Luther nailed his 95 theses to the Wittenberg Castle Church door in 1517.

WHAT IS BIBLICAL THEOLOGY?

We speak of a "rebirth" of Biblical Theology because it had been defined almost two centuries before. In 1787 a German theologian Gabler first used the term "Biblical Johann Theology" to distinguish his subject from systematic or dogmatic theology. Gabler's distinction was: "Biblical theology is historical in character and sets forth *what the sacred writers thought* about divine matters; dogmatic theology, on the contrary, is didactic in character, and teaches *what a particular theologian* philosophically and rationally *decides* about divine matters, in accordance with his character, .time, age, place, sect, or school."

The distinction resembles that between a newspaper reporter and a sociologist. Both may be interested in a riot, but they see it and deal with it differently. The reporter seeks details, trying to find exactly what happened in this particular riot. The sociologist is concerned with the riot as one of many, as an example of observable "laws," not as an individual phenomenon. The biblical theologian is like the reporter in that he is interested in the details of the theology of the particular books of the Bible. The systematic theologian is not interested in an individual book, or period, or author, but in formulating a general theology, like the "laws" of a sociologist, that will deal with the whole three thousand years of Judeo-Christian theological thought.

The object of Biblical Theology, therefore, is to set out what the writers of the Bible thought on the theological subjects that concerned them. Biblical Theology attempts to be a scientific procedure — one that operates with all the grammatical, historical, and literary tools provided by scholars in fields allied to biblical studies. Its task is descriptive, trying as far as possible to convey what the biblical writers would wish conveyed if they were asked what the essential message of their writing was.

Biblical Theology is a discipline that falls between the History of Religion and Systematic Theology. The History of Religion attempts to show the development of religion, concentrating on observable changes, on details that differ from one era to another. Systematic Theology concentrates on the accumulated wisdom of all theology from the past, trying to present a message that is the best of that theology. It attempts to systematize the thinking of the Church and make it understandable and appealing to the people of the present time.

Biblical Theology, in contrast to Systematic Theology, is not greatly concerned to appeal to modern man; rather it is concerned to be true to the biblical message. It is not concerned to be systematic, since the Bible is not really systematic. In contrast to the History of Religion, Biblical Theology is not greatly concerned to describe the changes in biblical religion, but rather to describe the basic biblical faith that has undergone these changes. It assumes that there is a certain amount of unity within the Testaments and between them, for this unity amidst diversity is one of the important facts about the Bible, as it is also a central fact in a close-knit family.

THE UNITY WITHIN THE BIBLE

No scholar denies that there is diversity within the Bible. The debated question is how much unity there is. Most books (and there have been many since 1930) entitled *Old Testament Theology* or *New Testament Theology* assume that there is a substantial unity within the Testaments, and the authors have attempted to present that unity so that their readers may know what "the faith of Israel" or "the faith of the earliest church" was.

These authors do not deny that expressions of these "faiths" vary, nor that there is at times direct contradiction. Their thesis is, however, that behind the varying expressions there is some basic agreement. In a similar way the Democratic party is comprised of various interest groups — labor, minorities, intellectuals, and the poor. Yet behind their diversity of interests there is unity of faith in the necessity and ability of government to be the chief force in eliminating the injustices of society. A political scientist can speak of "the faith of Democrats" just as a biblical theologian can speak of "the faith of the early church," even though its interests and expressions varied.

There is one *Theology of the New Testament*, that by Rudolph Bultmann, which disagrees with this basic view. This book is written in sections which attempt to show the development of theology in the early Church. Written in 1950, the book actually represents more accurately views of 1910 when Bultmann was a student. His interest in the varieties of theological expression in the early Church is not as widely shared as it once was. His presuppositions and conclusions are so different from scholars representing the "Biblical Theology" approach that it would merely complicate the issue to examine them here. The next chapter will consider his approach to the Bible. For a variety of other reasons also Bultmann stands out from biblical theologians like a black sheep in a white flock.

Not only is substantial unity seen in the diversity of each of the Testaments, but biblical theologians also claim that there is basic unity between the Old and New Testaments. In the nineteenth century, it was generally thought that the Old Testament was connected with the New only as the historical background for the thought of the Church. The theory of progress and development declared that there is essential disunity between the Testaments, especially since Jesus Christ was the center of only one Testament. Here, too, the view has changed, for the basic *structure* of the theology of the Old Testament is now seen as the same as that of the New Testament. This means that underlying all the writing of the two Testaments is faith in the living God who is active in history, revealing Himself to His people through His actions. That is the point of essential unity between the Testaments, and is the basic proclamation of the approach to the Bible called Biblical Theology.

GOD WHO ACTS

The Backbone of the Bible

"Biblical theologians' are those who claim that the central affirmation of the Bible is that God has acted in history, revealing Himself to man in His acts. The historical events in which God acted are said to be the backbone of the Bible, from the beginning of Israel to the time of the early Church. The central affirmations of the Bible are not those which speak of religion (what man does towards God), or of ethics (what man does towards his fellowman), but those that proclaim what *God* has done *towards man.*

This assertion that "the acts of God" are the backbone of the Bible is an interpretation, not a conclusion that is obvious to all readers of the Bible. In all literature some key to interpretation must be selected, for not all the material presented can be equally important. For example, the reader of *For Whom the Bell Tolls* must decide whether the center of Hemingway's interest lies in the love story, the war, or the bonds between the characters. The reader must choose his own key, justifying his choice by the help it gives him in unlocking the meaning of the work. This is especially true when a collection of writings is under consideration. The Jews chose "Law" as the key meaning of the Old Testament, but Paul claimed that "God's Promise" was the more basic element. Today, Paul's viewpoint is expanded so that promise and fulfillment of the promise are taken together by biblical theologians as God's acts in history, and called the basic element in the Bible. The next two chapters will present other answers to this same quest for the interpretive key to the Bible.

History and Miracle

When it is said that God acts *in history*, several important distinctions must be drawn. First, this is different from acting "in nature," in rain, crop growth, etc. Nature was the domain of most of the ancient gods, who were called "nature gods" because their only influence was thought to be upon "nature." The God of Israel acted in nature too, but His primary action was in the events of human history, especially in the history of Israel and of Jesus of Nazareth. It was this characteristic of acting in history that set Israel's God apart from almost all other gods of the ancient Orient, as a politician working in the United States Agricultural Department to change the laws must be distinguished from his brother who is interested only in his crops.

Secondly, to say that God has acted in history does not always mean a "miracle" has taken place. Sometimes God was believed to act in what we today call miraculous or supernatural events. The Bible, however, makes no distinction between natural and supernatural events, for all things were possible to God, and He acted as much in "normal" events as He did in miracles. When, for example, Rachel bore children, a normal event, it was said to have been the Lord's doing (Gen. 30:22). When Jesus was miraculously raised from the dead, that too was said to be because God had raised Him (Acts 2:24). If we are to understand the Bible, we must discard the distinction between "natural" and "supernatural," for God is understood to be involved with all of life, acting in, with, and behind the ordinary course of events. God is not basically a disaster relief agency that comes in only after an extraordinary event like a hurricane. Rather He is the Water Department that works quietly and unseen at all times and in all places.

The Role of the Prophet

A problem with this central theme of the Bible is: what does it mean to say that "God has acted in history and revealed Himself in His acts"? This is not the same kind of statement as, for example, "Jesus acted in history." No one disputes that, for Jesus was a particular man of a particular time about whom witnesses present a certain amount of information. But what kind of information could be presented as witness to the statement, "God has acted in history"?

Saying "God has acted" is an interpretation of some events of the past. In Israel's history and Jesus' life events took place which observers believed God had been involved in. We are also talking about "interpretation" when we say that "God has revealed Himself in His acts."

A prophet was always necessary to make this interpretation known to the people. Sometimes the prophet preceded the event: Moses went into Egypt and said God would rescue His people; when they escaped they were convinced that God had saved them because Moses had foretold it (though the extraordinary nature of the escape also helped convince them). He became identified to them as "the Lord your God who brought you out of Egypt." By the time Jerusalem was destroyed in 586 bc, Jeremiah had been proclaiming for years that God was going to punish Israel for its sins. When the event occurred, it seemed to be the fulfillment of what Jeremiah had prophesied and so his view was accepted as the truth. So also when it was accurately prophesied that appeasing Hitler would lead to war, later observers concluded that appeasement is the road to war.

Many times in the Old and New Testaments, however, an act took place which had not been prophesied beforehand. Still, the event was called an act of God if a prophet saw God's hand in it. Prophets were men who were given understanding of God and His way with the world. They were men to whom God directly revealed Himself so that they then could go and speak to the people about Him. The prophet pointed out the divine action, and often pointed out conclusions to be drawn about God from the event. In a similar vein American writers today are interpreting the U.S. landing of men on the moon as evidence of American know-how, tenacity, courage, patience, technical superiority and possibly even godliness.

Judging Prophets

Sometimes prophets said something was done by God which was not done by Him. That type of proclamation was gradually censored: either because no one believed it, or because those who handed down the prophets' words found the proclamation unacceptable and so deleted it. The writings collected in the Old Testament were kept by the disciples of prophets who studied them and came to understand themselves in the light of past events. Then they understood the reports of the past in the light of their new situations and new understanding of God. This method is circular, but is valuable, as its use by political scientists can attest. The politics of the past generation helps explain the present, but present experience also helps in understanding the past.

Christians still use this method. We read the New Testament and its understanding of the way God has acted in Christ, and then we reread the Old Testament in order to see whether it conforms to this highest revelation God has given of Himself. In some cases, for example in the destruction of cities and whole peoples, we can only conclude that the prophet was wrong (Josh. 6:17) in his interpretation that God commanded it. In most cases we can see that proclamations of what God did in Israel enhance our understanding of God and must be used if we are to understand what the New Testament intends us to know of God.

Usually in the Old Testament, it is said that God has acted because something good has resulted from the event. In the Exodus the good that resulted was that the people were rescued from Egypt. In the destruction of Jerusalem the good was that Israel was punished, and so they came to know that God is a holy God whose love for Israel could not be taken for granted.

The reason Israel looked upon good results as God's doing was two-fold. They understood God to be gracious, giving more good things to His people than they deserved. Secondly, they acknowledged their own weakness and inability to save themselves, and so gave to God the glory for anything good that was accomplished. If evil came, it was usually recognized as punishment, which was a good thing in the long run. Sometimes, however, unmitigated evil came, and then it was said that Satan had brought it, not God (Job 1).

One cannot demonstrate the biblical faith that God is active. Its only justification is that it offers insight into human experience for those who adopt it. If it is to be translated into sociological terms, this faith expresses the following conviction: there is a force for good at work within history, a force that is more than the intentions and decisions of individuals. Sometimes this force uses seemingly evil events to bring an ultimate good. At other times a power of evil that has not been overcome appears to be at work.

We have now examined the general characteristics of the approach called "Biblical Theology." The following outline, though brief and highly selective, represents some details of what Biblical Theology finds most important in the Bible.

THE ACTS OF GOD IN HISTORY

THE HISTORY OF ISRAEL

The Old Testament does not have a definition of God, at least not one that could be put into abstract philosophical or theological language. The Israelites understood God in terms of His acts. If a definition could be given of Him it would be, "I am the Lord your God who brought you out of the land of Egypt" (Ex. 20:2). These are the words that stand as the preamble to the Ten Commandments. They are the justification for giving the commandments, for they say that God has been gracious to Israel so that the response that is appropriate is a life outlined by these commandments.

Exodus: *The Birth of a Nation*

The Exodus created Israel, for it was here that its central characteristic, faith in Yahweh, originated (Yahweh was the name of Israel's God, a name used to distinguish Him from the gods other nations worshiped). No one can be absolutely sure what happened when Israel escaped from Egypt, for the accounts conflict somewhat. It seems clear that the people were led out by Moses who had told them that God would free them from Egypt. It is likely that some extraordinary events took place during the escape so that it seemed to be confirmed that God had rescued His people from bondage.

Whatever happened, the people who escaped believed that God had been instrumental in their escape. They may have heard Yahweh's name from their fathers while in Egypt (but they may not have also; the Bible is contradictory on this point), but they did not know of His gracious, rescuing, acting-in-history nature until their escape. The Exodus defined Him as much as He could be defined. All that happened in Israel's history thereafter refined the understanding that the Exodus created, as the last fifty years of Einstein's life were the working out and refining of the genius expressed in his Theory of Relativity when he was only twenty-six.

Many things were revealed to the people in the event of the Exodus, once they came to see God was active in it just as a child comes to know his father and himself much better when his father climbs up a tree in which his son is stuck and carries him down. Israel gradually recognized that God loved them, not because they deserved to be loved, but simply because He had chosen them in their fathers. They came to see that God keeps His covenant and so can be trusted. They also realized that God is the Great Power in the universe who must be reckoned with in history, for He will accomplish His will, even if the whole Egyptian nation tries to stand in His way. The Exodus taught much more about Yahweh also, but these three points were central and have remained the foundation for Israel's understanding of God ever since.

Exile: Dissolution and Destruction

The second crisis in Israel's history was the Exile, which

followed the destruction of Jerusalem by the Babylonians. Because of the graciousness of God towards Israel in the Exodus the people believed that He would rescue them no matter what they did. They believed that He needed them as His people just as much as they needed Him as their God.

This belief that God would never punish His people was assailed by the prophets from the eighth century onward, for they proclaimed that Yahweh demands ethical living, a holiness among His people that reflects His own holiness. When the people did not basically reform, the prophets announced that God would destroy the nation as punishment. This destruction began in 722 BC when the Assyrians overran the northern half of the nation. The final debacle happened in 586 BC when the Babylonians destroyed Jerusalem and deported most of the people.

When Jerusalem was conquered, nothing that we today would call supernatural occurred. Babylon had a great army, and great armies win wars. But Israel had been accustomed to being rescued by God whenever she was attacked by bigger armies; so when she was not rescued, she believed that God had forsaken her, as a juvenile delinquent thinks his parents have abandoned him when they refuse to bail him out of jail the third time he is arrested. Those who believed in Yahweh only for what He could bring, abandoned Him at this point because they thought He ought to have given them what they wanted. But Jeremiah and others (Isaiah 40-55) proclaimed that God had not abandoned His people, rather He was chastising them.

Out of this great crisis in Israel's history the people learned the second facet of God's nature: He is not only a gracious, loving, powerful God, but He is also a holy God who expects and demands of His people a reflection of His own character. In a similar way today students who have been disciplined for unruly conduct are coming to realize that the university not only gives, but also demands the acceptance of responsibility in accord with the tenets of an academic community. Israel came to see that they did not own Yahweh, as other nations thought they owned and controlled their gods. Rather Yahweh owned them, and it was His will, not theirs, that would be done.

Return: New Life for Dry Bones

Not only did Jeremiah and the prophets who preceded him proclaim that God would punish Israel, but they also said that He would rescue a remnant, a very small group, to form the nucleus of a new Israel. At the heart of this nucleus would be a new king like David, a son of David who would be holy, powerful, filled with God's Spirit. Even amidst the dark hours of Jerusalem's destruction this promise was on the lips of the prophets. Ezekiel expressed this hope in a vision of a valley full of dry bones that were brought back to life by the Spirit of God blowing over them.

The prophet's faith in the future depended on Israel's knowledge of God. They knew that God would fulfill His covenant with the nation, not destroying it completely, but raising up a seedling which would be His new people. During the exile in Babylon this theme was taken up by an anonymous prophet known as Second Isaiah (Isaiah 40-55). He proclaimed great hopes for the future: God would rescue His people a second time from the grip of a powerful enemy, returning them to the land of Canaan. There they would become the center of a world-wide mission to bring all nations to worship Yahweh. This new call to Israel is like the call the United States has heard in this generation — to be the bread basket for all the world's hungry, instead of sitting back and enjoying God's gift of abundance, unconcerned for others.

A portion of Israel returned to her own land in 538-7 BC, but on nothing like the grand scale prophesied by Second Isaiah. God rescued His people from Babylon through Cyrus the Persian, but most of the great hopes for an Israelite renaissance did not come to fruition then, and so the people continued to look to the future. In the return from Babylon they learned that God had not abandoned them forever, but had remembered His covenant and continued to act graciously to His people. They learned also that God's time was not their time, that they could not know when God would consummate His desires for the world. They just had to wait. In our world today the United Nations is such a return (to the League of Nations idea) and promise, giving us hope for world peace through law. But we have to wait for the promise to come to consummation.

Creation: The Beginning of It All

Second Isaiah based his confidence in God's great deed of the future on the faith that He was the Lord of all the earth, and Creator of all things that exist. By using Assyria and Babylon to punish Israel, He demonstrated that His action was not limited to Israel, for He acted through other nations also. Gradually the people realized that He was not simply the God of Israel, but was sovereign over the whole world.

This was not entirely new, for Amos had proclaimed it in the eighth century, and Moses had learned it in the Exodus. But the people had not fully accepted it, and the prophets had not emphasized it before the Exile. During the Exile, however, Second Isaiah presented the Old Testament's highest understanding of Yahweh, for he proclaimed that He is Creator of all, so that there are no other gods beside Him. Israel's growth to the awareness of the oneness of divinity resembles the growing understanding created by modern communications in the twentieth century — the world is one. The previous view that each nation is alone and completely sovereign is giving way to the realization that every nation is involved with and dependent on others. Mankind is one.

This emphasis on God the Creator is the fourth major theme of a Biblical Theology of the Old Testament. Creation cannot be called an act "in" history, for it is not an event that was observed by anyone. In one sense it is the beginning of history, or the presupposition of history, but it was not the beginning of Israel's understanding of Yahweh. They did not start asking how or when the world began, or who created it, and then concluding that there must be a Creator. They started, rather, with the events of their own history.

The Creation stories given in Genesis are not the oldest part of the Bible, for they come from the ninth century (Genesis 2) and the sixth century (Gen. 1). They are pictorial means of conveying Israel's knowledge of God that came through the events of her history. While Creation cannot be called an event "in history," it can be, and indeed was, understood as one of Yahweh's great acts.

The four great themes of the Old Testament, then, are these: Creation, Exodus, Exile, and Return. Israel's basic understanding of God is contained in His action proclaimed in these events. *Creation*: God is the supreme power in the world, ordering nature and history as He desires; *Exodus*: God is loving and gracious to His people, rescuing them when they are helpless and undeserving; *Exile*: God is holy, demanding that His people be true to Him, reflecting in their lives His own moral character; *Return*: no matter what His people have done, God is forgiving, taking back to Himself a remnant and promising a great salvation in the future.

THE NEW TESTAMENT

The New Testament picks up where the Old Testament leaves off, for it builds on these four understandings of God. There is no doubt that the Old Testament is a book without an ending. Not all the promises of God given to His people had been fulfilled by Jesus' time. Israel had not been rescued from the ravages of the nations. Rather, since the Exile she had been subjected to Persian, Greek, and Roman domination, with only a short time of independence. The great king like

David had not appeared, let alone the almost supernatural figure that some of the promises seemed to foretell (Isaiah 9, 11, 50, 53). For four hundred years preceding the birth of Christ Israel seemed to have been a backwater, a nation forgotten by God, a civilization in decline from its great days politically under David, and spiritually under the great prophets.

The New Testament takes up the unfulfilled promise and makes it the center of its proclamation. Jesus preached, "The time is fulfilled, the kingdom of God is at hand" (Mark 1:15). The "time" was the time of the great event that had been promised; the "kingdom" was the reign of God under His regent, the new king like David who would rescue His people from their sins. The message of the New Testament is that in the birth, death, and resurrection of Jesus this "time" and this "kingdom" have come.

The New Testament lays great stress upon God's action in history, in this case in the history of Jesus and the early Church, which can again be summarized in four great events: the Incarnation (coming in the flesh) of the Son of God; His death and resurrection for the salvation of mankind; the sending of the Holy Spirit; the Consummation of history which is promised shortly. Let us look briefly at each of these events to see how they were understood as acts of God in history.

Incarnation: Promise Fulfilled

The birth of Jesus was not understood simply to be a natural event without a message. Rather, the New Testament saw it as the act of God. Matthew and Luke make this point clear by saying that He was conceived by the action of God's Holy Spirit. John stresses God's action even more by saying that Jesus was the Word of God, the "reason" of God, which became flesh. Mark emphasizes that Christ is God's "beloved Son." Paul calls Him "the image of the invisible God," and Hebrews calls him God's agent in creation. The whole New Testament proclaims that the birth of Jesus was not simply a birth like other births, but was an act of God in which He set about fulfilling His promises that had been made through Israel's prophets.

Most of the references to Jesus do not stress that there was anything unusual about the circumstances of His birth. Matthew and Luke are the exceptions to this, for they report that angels were involved, and claim that His mother was a virgin at the time of his birth.

Even if the virgin birth took place, this is not the central act of God, or even proof of it. The great Act is not that Christ was born of a virgin, but that He was the Son of God incarnate (from the Latin "in" = in, "carne" = flesh). Believing in the Incarnation is an interpretation of the birth of Jesus, not a witness to observable facts. Even if it had been medically demonstrated at the time that Mary was a virgin who had conceived, this would not prove the New Testament assertions about Jesus. In the Old Testament it was said that Isaac was conceived because "the Lord visited Sarah . . . and . . . did to Sarah as he had promised" (Gen. 21:1), yet Isaac was not supernatural because of the manner of his conception. External facts never can prove, they can only point to, internal meaning. The facts, even if they include a supernatural birth, do not speak for themselves, just as the facts of the Exodus did not speak for themselves. There had to be a prophet who said that this man Jesus came from God. The primary prophet was Jesus Himself, who said that in Himself the promises of the Old Testament were being fulfilled, and called men to follow Him.

Once we learn that in Jesus of Nazareth we are confronted by an act of God, indeed by God Himself, then there is much that we come to understand about God. If God is like Jesus, then we see that God is One who forgives the sinner who repents, suffers with those who are in pain, loves all those who have need of Him, and gives Himself to the utmost for our welfare. If God has revealed Himself in Jesus, then the Gos-

pels convey to us what God is like and how we can expect Him
to act in our lives today.

Death and Resurrection: Man's Judgment and Re-Creation

The second great act of God in the New Testament is
Jesus' death and resurrection. The Incarnation was God's coming to man, making Himself known. In Jesus' death and resurrection God acted to rescue His people from their sins to recreate their broken lives. Jesus did not die merely because His
enemies were more powerful than He. He died because it was
the will of God that it should happen and so Jesus did not
maneuver to avoid a clash. Jesus told His disciples that He
"had to suffer" (Mark 8:31), for this was the will of God. And
so He died, giving His life as "a ransom for many" (Mark 10:
45), dying "for our sins" (1 Cor. 15:3), "putting away sin by
the sacrifice of Himself" (Heb. 9:26). The evidence for this
interpretation of Jesus' death, for once again this is interpretation, was found in the resurrection.

The Jews had proclaimed that Jesus was a sinner because He
advocated disobedience to some of the laws of the Old Testament. They said that He was cursed by God because He died
a criminal's death. The disciples were ready to accept that
theory on Good Friday, but on Easter their understanding of
what had happened changed completely, for they believed that
He was alive, that God had raised Him from the dead.

If there is one central event in the New Testament, it is
the resurrection. If there is one extraordinary happening that
cannot be removed without the whole edifice of New Testament Christianity being radically changed, it is the belief in
the resurrection of Jesus. The resurrection was the message
the apostles preached. The resurrection was the proof to them
that Jesus was approved by God, and not cursed by Him as His
death might indicate. Without the resurrection faith there
would have been no gospel and no Church (1 Cor. 15:14-19),

just as without the faith that "all men are created equal" there would have been no United States of America as it is known today.

Here again, the proclamation, "God has raised Him from the dead," was an interpretation that the apostles gave the facts they observed. They observed Him dead and buried, and then observed Him alive again. They thought it impossible that He could raise Himself, or that any other human being could raise Him, and so they proclaimed that God had raised Him from the dead and had given Him a place at His right hand. As the Exodus is the center of the faith of Israel, so the Resurrection is the center of the faith of the Church: "God has acted in history, raising Jesus from the dead, and of that we are all witnesses."

Inspiration: Birth of a New People

The first great event, the Incarnation, was the fulfillment of the promise to send a great Son of David to be king in Israel (Is. 9:6f., Jer. 23:5). The second great event, Jesus' death and resurrection, was God's action to fulfill the promise to make a new covenant with His people in which He would forgive their sins (Jer. 31:31-34, Is. 53:10-12). The third great event, the giving of the Holy Spirit at Pentecost (Acts 2), was the fulfillment of a third promise in which God said, "I will pour out my Spirit on all mankind" (Joel 2:28).

This third event was really the beginning of the Church and its mission, as Luther's experience of God's grace was the beginning of Protestantism. The disciples had been told by the Risen Christ to remain in Jerusalem until the Holy Spirit came upon them (Acts 1:4f.). In the story in Acts 2 the Holy Spirit is manifested by tongues of flame resting on all the Christians in the room, and then by their ability to speak in foreign languages which the visitors to Jerusalem from other nations were able to understand. This great event is told in Acts as the first time the Spirit came upon the apostles and followers of Jesus.

The rest of the New Testament accents that the Holy Spirit had indeed come upon the Church, and that Christians 'were guided by this inner moving of God, but the story of Pentecost is not referred to as the basis or proof of this.

There can be no doubt that the presence and power of the Holy Spirit (sometimes called the Spirit of God, or the Spirit of Christ) is a central theme of the New Testament. It is promised in the Gospels (Mark 1:8, etc.) and almost all the writers of Epistles had experienced a change in their lives which they attributed to the coming of the Spirit. The meaning of the gift of the Spirit was an acknowledgment that the understanding and love found in the Church were not human achievements but divine gifts. Secondly, the Spirit was understood as Christ Himself present in the Church, continuing to save and lead his followers.

Consummation: The Goal of History

The final event described in the New Testament is the Consummation, the End of the World, which is promised but not reached. This too is in line with Old Testament promises which speak of the resurrection of the dead, and the judgment of mankind (Dan. 12:2). Jesus' resurrection is the foretaste of this great event, the beginning of the resurrection of all. The Consummation is the final occurrence towards which the prophets of the Old Testament looked, and it is begun but not completed in Christ.

It is clear that the early Church believed that this consummation was imminent. They believed that Jesus taught that it would take place within a generation (Mark 9:1), but as the generation passed and the end of the world did not come, it was put off to the distant future (2 Pet. 3:8). But it still remained as an essential part of the framework of the faith of the New Testament. There was still evil in the world, and God's redemption could not be complete until evil was destroyed and a new heaven and a new earth brought forth out of the old. It remained a hope, and completed the Church's understanding of God. As in the beginning God had created the world, so at the end He would bring it to a conclusion.

The United States lives in hope of a consummation also. The beginning of the nation was the declaration of universal human equality, but so far that has never been achieved here. We have come to see that minorities and the poor are never given an equal start, so now the nation is attempting to change, to eliminate the built-in discrimination in The System. The goals toward which the nation is aiming is the day when all American children will be born with an equal opportunity to develop their talents. That end has been promised for generations, and steps toward it have been taken. But the Declaration of Equality, like God's declaration of the goodness of creation, remains only a promise whose day has not yet arrived.

Thus we find Biblical Theology claiming that the central message of the Bible is enshrined in the great acts of God. The beginning and the end, the Creation and the Consummation, are not really events of history, but are the beginning and end of history. They are not reported as occurrences which men witness, report, and interpret. They are mythical "supra-historical" events which enshrine the faith of Israel and the Church: if God is the Lord of history, He must also be the Beginning and End of history.

Between these two mythical book ends are lined the six central historical events of the Bible, the backbone of the story, by which the rest holds together and must be understood. These are the Exodus, Exile, and Return of Israel; the Incarnation, Death, and Resurrection of Jesus, and the sending of the Holy Spirit upon the Church. If we understand these events, what was perceived in them, what legends arose from them, etc., we have an essential grasp of the meaning of the Bible. Everything else flows from them. So say the Biblical Theologians.

Evaluation

IMPOSED UNITY

There are basically three challenges raised to this approach. The first asserts that the assumed unity of the Bible is really imposed on it by biblical theologians. Those who adopt a narrowly historical approach charge that the essential characteristic of the Bible is its diversity, not its unity, and the proper way to understand it is as a progression from more primitive to more mature religious expression.

There is no doubt that there is truth in the claim that the Bible enshrines progress. Each of the great acts of God described above built on something old and convinced the people of something new that had not been sufficiently emphasized before. The historians are right in pointing to a theological evolution, and biblical theologians agree. Whether or not the historians are right in denying that there is also an essential unity of faith in the Lord of history is a question that each reader must decide after reading the evidence we have presented.

Deciding whether or not there is an essential unity within the diversity of the Bible is like trying to determine whether a particular hypothesis about United States history is true. It could be claimed that a central unifying theme of that history is violence, as described in the report of the President's Violence Commission. The skeleton of the story would be our nine wars. Then the flesh of the theory would be made of Indian slaughter, frontier vengeance, cruelty to slaves, lynchings, race riots, labor riots, assassinations, and a fantastic murder rate. As it is difficult to discern if there is such a unity in violence in the history of the United States of America, so also it is not easy to decide whether there is a unity in God's action in the biblical history.

NARROW VISION?

The second objection raised to Biblical Theology is that the interpretive key, "God's acts in history," is inadequate. It is asserted that this may be an important motif, but others ought not to be neglected in presenting what the Bible actually says. For example, it is claimed that the Jews cannot be entirely wrong in seeing "Law," in the sense of ethical imperatives as a central issue in both Testaments. Books like Proverbs and James have little to do with history but a great deal to do with man's ethical life. Another important motif is worship, for the Psalms are filled with an emphasis on worship but have very little interest in history.

Undoubtedly, there are these other emphases that must be included in any Biblical Theology. The approach presented here can include them, showing how each is dependent upon the primary motif. But when either of the others is taken as the key, God's involvement in history usually becomes an embarrassment and so is neglected as it was by Judaism in Paul's time and Liberalism in the last century. If an interpretation using "Law" as the key could be presented to make sense of the whole of the Bible, then it would clamor for attention. None has yet been provided, for the difficulties are too great.

NONSENSE

The third objection that is raised to this approach is that the concept of God acting in history is primitive mythology that is nonsense to modern man and so must be the husk rather than the kernel of biblical truth. This is the most important of the charges made, and is the basic issue in the debate about Demythologizing to which we must now turn.

8

The Mythical Language of the Bible

Demythologizing. The word itself is enough to raise the fear that some German theologian safe in his ivory tower has taken a knife to the Bible and is attempting to dismember it. The word does have a technical ring, and was coined by a German theologian, Rudolph Bultmann. But he was not safe in an ivory tower when he publicized his views. Rather, he was a prominent member of the German Confessing Church that was then (1941) opposing Hitler. And Bultmann himself had no intention of dismembering the Bible. Instead, he was searching for its deepest meaning, a message of monumental relevance to the desperate situation of his day.

This whole chapter will concentrate on understanding and evaluating the demythologizing approach to the Bible, for modern biblical interpretation cannot be understood without it. Between the World Wars Karl Barth and Biblical Theology ruled the theological world. But Bultmann opposed a number of the essential characteristics of that approach and apparently spoke for many others when he did so. For from 1941 to about 1960 Bultmann and Demythologizing were the center of most of the ferment of theology. In the 1960's there have been a number of new directions taken, but they all in some way depend on Bultmann.

Certain facets of the Biblical Theology approach have now been adopted by almost all scholars. Likewise certain facets of the Demythologizing approach have come to be almost universally accepted. It is necessary to understand this approach, therefore, because it is one of the foundation stones of interpretation of the Bible today.

Bultmann's Viewpoint

Bultmann's position is a synthesis of the Liberalism which concentrated on the Bible as Literature and History, and the Biblical Theology which was the subject of the last chapter. Bultmann was a student at the height of Liberalism, around the turn of the century. From his schooling he adopted the view that miracles are impossible, that God cannot act in the world to interfere with the normal, outward course of events.

But Bultmann also came to see, with Barth and the biblical theologians, that the central message of the Bible is that God has acted in Jesus Christ. Bultmann's theology attempts to say that God has acted, but not in the way the Bible often says, in the outward course of events, in miracles. "Demythologizing" attempts to say that God's action is always hidden and known only to the eye of faith.

THE CRUX OF THE MATTER

Mythology Defined

The key to Bultman's thought is his definition of mythology as a primitive conception of the world which differs radically from the understanding developed by the scientific method.

Before modern science arose many people believed that supernatural figures interrupted the smooth flow of nature. They believed that gods, angels, spirits, and demons were agents who interfered in the natural course of events and caused inexplicable phenomena.

Science has found that dismissing the possibility of supernatural interference has greatly enhanced knowledge of the world. Once the theory that demons caused sickness was put to one side, it became possible to discover germs. Scientists can find no observable, measurable evidence of supernatural invasions of nature, so they feel justified in assuming that they do not happen. Doctors act this same way in concluding that there is nothing physically wrong with a complaining patient if all tests are negative.

Scientists assume that the universe is a unified, self-enclosed system in which everything that happens within the system can be explained by something else in it. Bultmann adopts this viewpoint, claiming that it is the only one possible for modern man who has been indoctrinated in scientific thinking since his birth. He concludes that biblical statements about God, angels, and other powers interferring in the natural course of events must not be taken literally. He calls such statements mythology.

Mythology Incarnate

Mythology speaks of God as if He were a factor to be considered in the events of the natural, physical world, whereas God is not a part of the natural world. Mythology speaks of God naively, as if He were a cause like other causes in the world, only stronger. It pictures God acting the same way a man acts, except that since He is invisible, His involvement is not as obvious. In particular mythology points to extraordinary events, the parting of the Red Sea or Jesus' resurrection, and says that the only possible explanation of them is that they are miracles, that God has overruled natural law by His own immediate power.

Mythology, according to Bultmann, has a conception of God that is similar to that which many people hold of the Federal Government. Most of the time our daily life goes along its natural course with no interference from Washington. But every so often, especially at tax time, Uncle Sam makes an appearance, sticking his hand in our pockets. Likewise, in the mythological view, God is outside the natural world of cause and effect but every so often He interferes when He wants to change something.

In particular Bultmann points to the New Testament and says that most of the theological statements about Jesus are examples of the mythological way of speaking. A divine being coming to earth and dying as a sacrifice for sin is mythology. The resurrection of a dead man, His ascension to heaven, and the hope for His return on wings of clouds also represent the primitive point of view that there are divine interventions in nature that are observable to men.

Bultmann believes that God acted in Jesus, but says that speaking of outward, visible divine acts makes it impossible for modern man to share that belief. What is needed, according to Bultmann, is some way to express the meaning of God's action in Jesus, while not tying it to the primitive, mythological form in which it is found in the New Testament. Finding this expression is the task of Demythologizing.

INTERPRETATION NOT ELIMINATION

An attempt was made by nineteenth century Liberalism to deal with the mythology of the Bible, but it failed. Liberalism did not understand the gospel, for it thought that Jesus was essentially a teacher of religious and ethical truths that man just needed to learn in order to change himself. The assertion that God had acted in Jesus was rejected by Liberalism, so naturally the mythological descriptions of this action were rejected also. The mythology was eliminated as worthless. Bultmann declares that this approach was wrong, for New Testament mythology does have something important to say to us today, so it should not be eliminated. Instead, it must be interpreted.

Liberalism approached the mythology of the New Testament like a prose writer who does not understand poetry. Because he does not think and write that way himself he assumes that poetry is just jibberish, as if monkeys had played with typewriters. Not understanding it, he throws it out. But it can be understood and interpreted by someone who knows what poetry is and how to explain its meaning.

True Appreciation

We can interpret myths when we understand what they mean and why they were written. Myth, according to Bultmann, is a means of conveying an understanding of personal life, an answer to the question, "Who am I?" Mythology expresses man's belief that the world and personal life are riddled with mysteries. Myths about gods and demons express the belief that there is a limit beyond man, that there is a power beyond him which he cannot calculate or control.

Mythology speaks about this power beyond man inadequately and improperly because it speaks about it as if it were worldly, physical power. It speaks of God as if He were a power like other visible "empirical" powers in the world, but in truth He is an invisible, "existential" power that cannot be observed or measured. This confusion of two similar but distinct entities is like a child describing God as if He were his earthly, visible father.

It is very important to see here the distinction Bultmann makes between empirical (physical) and existential (spiritual) powers. Empirical powers are those which are visible and measurable so that a scientific observer could view them objectively and describe them. Gravity is such an empirical power. Existential powers are not visible or measurable, but they are real powers that are only known by experiencing them, for they influence our personal life. Love is such an existential power. It cannot be measured or proven to exist. It can only be known by experiencing it. Empirical powers act *upon us* in the same way they act upon inanimate objects. Existential powers act *within us*, in our own experience of being human, in a way that is completely different from the action of empirical, measurable powers. These existential powers may be natural, like love, or supernatural, like God, their common quality being that they can only be known by experience.

Mythology, in Bultmann's view, is speaking of supernatural, existential powers as if they were empirical, measurable forces acting in the world in an observable manner. In the Bible, for example, there are stories of demons which physically cause men to go into convulsions. There are also stories of the Holy Spirit acting physically upon men and making them speak in foreign languages. These are forces acting upon man, creating observable effects, just as natural forces like germs act upon man. Bultmann says that modern man cannot accept this idea that there are supernatural forces which act upon man in a physical manner just as natural forces act upon him.

The Powers That Be

On the other hand, Bultmann believes that modern man can believe in supernatural powers that act upon man as existential forces in his personal experience. Man knows that there are not just natural, empirical forces in the world, for he knows that there are powers beyond him, that limit him and to some degree determine his life. Modern man does not greatly object to the concept of a power of evil in the world, as it is seen in a mob or in a nation that turns from being peaceful to wishing to conquer its neighbors. Nationalism is an existential force, sometimes for good, sometimes for evil.

Not only does modern man realize that there are existential powers at work in the world, he also recognizes that there are such powers at work within himself. Man knows that within himself there is a power of evil that leads him to do evil even when he wants to do good. As long as these powers are not described as forces acting physically upon him, as demons were supposed to do, then modern man has no objection. In fact, according to Bultmann, when the New Testament speaks of demons, what it really wants to speak about is the power of evil within man, but it did not make the distinction between empirical and existential powers. So Bultmann demythologizes the concept of demons by saying that they represent the personal powers of evil within man. In almost the same way a psychiatrist has to interpret dreams, which are outward pictures of an inner reality. A woman dreamed continually that her husband chopped her head off: the psychiatrist "demythologized" her dream by suggesting this expressed her constant experience of him making her feel inferior and so depriving her of her personal worth.

Mythology, according to Bultmann, is speaking of existential powers, in particular God, as if they were empirical powers acting visibly within the world. Biblical myths, which speak of God acting visibly and objectively like gravity, really want to say that God acts invisibly within man like love and is known only by faith, by experiencing His presence.

Mythology is thus an outward symbol of an inner reality, exactly as the sacrament of the Lord's Supper is an outward symbol of an inner experience. Bultmann does not want to eliminate the myth. He wants to interpret it so that the inner reality it means to express, not the outward means of expressing it, becomes the center of attention.

THE PERSONAL MESSAGE OF THE NEW TESTAMENT

Man's Dilemma

The tool which Bultmann uses to interpret the New Testament is Existentialist Philosophy. He finds that the categories that are used in this philosophy express the assumptions on the nature of man better than any other philosophy. Existentialism describes life without faith as a life dependent on the visible world, attempting to find security in that which is observable. Since this tangible, visible sphere of life is transitory, the man who bases his life on it becomes the prisoner and slave of corruption. His foundation just passes away, as the suicides by businessmen during the Depression proclaimed.

In addition, when we depend on this visible sphere we collide with other people, for there is only so much material to be spread around. We seek our own security at the expense of other people, and thus envy, anger, jealousy, and hatred arise. But man cannot find the kind of security he seeks and thus he becomes the slave of anxiety, and anxiety leads to despair, which leads to death. Two brothers who both aspire to the leadership of their father's company will often fight to the bitter end to achieve their goal. But winning is no better than losing, for only power and money are gained while a brother and the security of a relationship of partners has been lost. This is what is meant by "gaining the whole world and losing your self."

On the other hand, this philosophy describes true life, which, for the Christian, is the life of faith. This is life that is dependent upon the unseen, intangible reality of God who confronts us as love. Faith means giving up our attempts to carve out a niche in life for ourselves, surrendering all our self-confidence and resolving to trust in God alone. We thus become detached from the world and independent of it.

A man of faith is able to treat those "two imposters, Success and Failure," just the same — with indifference. His life is filled with his relationships with others, with the Love which is the presence of the Other. There is no competition in this sphere, only cooperation. There is no defeat because God will be victorious.

God's Solution

The great question is: how can man change from a man without faith to being a man with faith? Existentialist philosophy believes that man can make that move simply by his own knowledge of himself and his decision to change. Bultmann, on the other hand, says that man is lost in his life without faith and cannot change himself.

The Existentialists are optimists, believing that "man is the master of his fate, the captain of his soul." Bultmann adopts the realism of the Bible, however, recognizing and proclaiming that man cannot change himself simply by deciding to. If modern psychology has accented any one central discovery, it is that the forces that operate within man are too deep and too strong to be controlled simply by man's will. If freedom is to come to trapped and frightened man, it must come from outside him. Bultmann says that such freedom is God's act in Christ's cross.

The New Testament understands the cross, according to Bultmann, in a mythological manner, for it speaks of a divine, preexistent figure who came to earth and suffered for the sins of other men; it speaks of this divine man offering his life as a sacrifice for others. Bultmann calls this primitive mythology. But while this detailed interpretation of the cross is not acceptable to modern man, it is clear that the cross is an event of history. Jesus Christ did indeed die, and throughout the history of the Church the proclamation of His death upon the cross has been the center of the gospel and the means to new life for millions of people.

Liberating Condemnation

Bultmann claims that the death of Jesus Christ upon the cross is an event which affects the whole of humanity in its relationship to God, for the Cross judges men and so frees them. The Cross is the judgment of God upon all mankind, condemning them and showing them that they are sinners who cannot save themselves. If this message gets across to man through preaching so that he understands himself as a helpless sinner, then he will, by confessing his helplessness, become reborn because of God's quite unmerited mercy.

The first part of this theory that the Cross is God's judgment on mankind is stated in the New Testament (Rom. 8:3) and almost universally believed in the Church. It is a common experience in the history of man's execution of martyrs. The death of Socrates at the hands of his fellow Athenians in 399 BC has turned out to be a condemnation of them, not of Socrates, in the eyes of history.

The second link in this understanding of the Cross is confusing, for Bultmann never makes completely clear how he thinks this judgment brings new life to the man who has no faith. His view appears to be that man needs to recognize his plight and will thereby be enabled to decide to become a man of faith. God's gift in the Cross, then, is the convincing information to man that he is a slave. Once man recognizes this he can believe in Christ and so be free of his dependence on the world.

The Resurrection Myth

While the death of Jesus Christ on the Cross is an historical event that we can know about, Bultmann believes that the resurrection is not an historical event but is simply the New Testament's way of conveying the meaning of the Cross. It was the disciples' attempt to proclaim that the Cross of Christ is an event that has meaning for all of mankind for all time. Proclaiming the resurrection of Christ is a mythological means of saying that His death is not just an ordinary human death but is the judgment and salvation of the world. It is an attempt to say that His death by itself was the victory over the power of death. As the legend of King Arthur is a means of conveying English medieval views of chivalry so, according to Bultmann, the myth of the resurrection is the biblical means of proclaiming the Christian understanding of salvation.

We come to believe in the Cross of Christ only through the preaching of the Church. Christ meets us in this proclamation as One crucified and risen. He meets us in this word of preaching and nowhere else. The word of preaching confronts us as the Word of God and we are not to ask why it so confronts us, anymore than we can ask why the policeman confronts us and demands obedience. It is we who are questioned by preaching's call to faith and are not allowed to question back.

THE ACT OF GOD IN CHRIST

One standard objection to the theology of Bultman is that, though he tries to demythologize all the other acts of God, he will not demythologize the final act of God in Jesus Christ for mankind's salvation. Bultmann, however, denies that this is mythology as he defines mythology. In mythological thinking God intervenes in natural or historical events. For example, a miracle is the effect of a supernatural cause, so that there is no natural cause by which it can be explained.

Hidden

But Bultmann does not understand God's act in Jesus Christ to be this kind of mythological event. God's act in Jesus Christ happens not between worldly events so that it can be observed as a necessary link, but hidden *within* them. His act is not visible; it cannot be seen or deduced as if it were a necessary cause in the chain of events. Rather the action of God is hidden behind the events and is visible only to the eye of faith.

Modern, secular man admits that there are spiritual forces at work in the world. Religious man goes beyond that general statement and says specifically that God is the great power for good that man experiences. Christian man, however, by the eye of faith, goes even further than this general statement about God, for he claims that in Jesus Christ, and in the present preaching of the Cross, God acted and continues to act to save men.

Effective

Today, God acts by leading men to believe in Christ when they hear the Cross preached. God acts within man, convincing them of the truth of the message preached. That message says that life can only be received by abandoning dependence on the visible, and casting one's self upon God as Christ did when He accepted the Cross. For Bultmann, the fact that men today believe the gospel is the one great miracle. For the gospel is not logical and reasonable, but is a stumbling block, foolishness, when viewed coldly and analytically. Nevertheless, men believe, and find new life in believing. This happens because they are confronted by God in the preaching of the Cross, as many Americans were confronted by the Absolute Imperative of equality for all men when they heard Martin Luther King preach "I Have a Dream."

Thus, when Bultman speaks of God acting, he means God acts as an existential force, invisibly, within events. He does not mean God acts as an empirical power, out in the open so that man can see and observe Him. Bultmann speaks of God's action as similar to our actions in human relationships, when we personally influence each other. Saying "God acts," means that in the preaching of the gospel we are confronted by God, addressed, questioned, judged, or blessed by Him. We cannot prove this, but this is what we understand has happened to us when the word of preaching comes to us.

This does not mean that God has no objective reality outside our faith. It also does not mean that He acts only within individuals and didn't act in the history of Jesus Christ. The Word of God that is proclaimed in the preaching was not invented by man, but had its origin in an historical event. This historical event of the death of Jesus Christ was the beginning of the preaching which brings us redemption and new life now. Therefore, we can say that the figure and work of Jesus Christ are to be understood as the divine work of redemption.

EVALUATION

There are many good points to Bultmann's understanding. In the first place, it stresses the heart of the New Testament message that God has acted in Christ. This is a great advance over much of the understanding of Liberalism and of the Church today. These see Jesus as an ethical teacher, one who tells us the way we ought to live, implying we can do it if we will try. Bultmann, on the other hand, proclaims that the heart of the gospel message is that man can only live as God intended him to live through God's act in Christ. The slave cannot free himself, he must have an emancipator.

In the second place, Bultmann's interpretation of the New Testament brings out the present relevance of the gospel. Bultmann makes clear that it applies to man in his present situation. He emphasizes that man must make a decision by himself — either the decision of faith to believe in Jesus Christ and accept the redemption that God offers to him, or the decision not to live by faith but reject God's offer of salvation. Every man is given a way out of his servitude, but some refuse freedom and the responsibility it brings, preferring to "bear the ills we have, than to fly to those we know not of."

This is an important addition to the Biblical Theology that was discussed in the last chapter. That viewpoint could allow a man to look at the Bible as merely a description of what God has done in the past. But Bultmann wishes to emphasize that the Bible is primarily concerned with the present, using the past to convince us that we must say "Yes" or "No" to God in the present. Bultmann is stamping across every page of the New Testament three words — "This Concerns You."

In the third place, Bultmann points out the Church's task in interpreting the New Testament. Modern man does not understand much of the New Testament. Bultmann accurately stresses the importance of distinguishing between what man is called on to believe today and what is the mythology of the past. In particular, Bultmann emphasizes what is really the central question of all Christian thought: "In what way has God acted in the past and how does he act today?" By focusing on this question, Bultmann has stimulated theological debate among Christians. His answer, however, is open to several objections.

MYTH TOO BROADLY DEFINED

Red Herrings

Bultmann applies the word "myth" far too broadly. Not all the stories and ideas he calls myths can helpfully be viewed in the same category. By refusing to allow Bultmann to include disparate types of material under the heading of myth we can eliminate many of the red herrings in the dispute and get down to the real issues.

In the first place, the picturesque descriptions of creation and consummation that are found especially in the books of Genesis and Revelation are myths in the traditional literary sense, and so Bultmann's demythologizing is the proper method for interpreting them. These are stories about the beginning and end of time and speak of God acting when no man was there to observe. In general, these literary myths are not greatly disputed. Most scholars do demythologize them in order to present the central message they proclaim, as Bultmann suggests should be done.

In the second place, other ideas that Bultmann calls myths are really symbols. The three-story view of the universe is a good example. Not even in the time of the New Testament did people believe that God was enthroned in heaven apart from man on earth. They believed that God was everywhere. But they *pictured* God as enthroned in order to say that he was sovereign, transcendent, beyond man. Likewise, hell is a symbol of the great power of evil, which again and again afflicts mankind. These biblical symbols serve the same kind of purpose that "John Bull" or "Uncle Sam" do. While we do not have to continue using traditional symbols, they do help to express realities.

Thirdly, some events that Bultmann calls myths are really statements of faith. In this category are invisible divine actions, when God does not intervene in the natural course of events. The New Testament assertion that Jesus was God incarnate is such a statement of faith. The incarnation is not an act that could be proved or disproved by scientific observation, for it took place in the birth of a child. There are details in the birth narratives of Matthew and Luke that are mythical in Bultmann's sense of observable divine interventions — the angels are the best examples. But the presence or absence of the angels is not essential to the Incarnation. They are added to emphasize the magnitude of the event taking place in silence in Bethlehem. Jesus was a man like other men and yet the Church asserts by faith that God Himself was present in Him.

If the New Testament view had been that "the Son of Man came down from heaven" like an angel dropping in on the earth, having no human parents or history, then this would be mythology. But the New Testament points to a man whose parents and birthplace and history were known and observed as fairly ordinary and certainly completely human. Though nothing too extraordinary took place in His life, still His followers came to the conclusion that in meeting Him they had met God. The Incarnation is not myth, but is a statement of faith, as the assertion that the United States is the world's great land of opportunity is a statement of faith.

The Real Issue

A fourth kind of story exactly fits Bultmann's definition of myth, for these are miraculous divine actions in which God is said to intervene in the natural course of events. The best example is the resurrection of Jesus. Here was a man who had died. His body was presumably in the process of decay. And yet the New Testament claims that His body was brought back to life so that on Easter morning the tomb was empty and He was seen again by His disciples.

It is said expressly throughout the New Testament that God had raised Him from the dead, and it was believed that this action opposed the way things usually happen. It was an action that happened right in the midst of the normal course of events, reversing that normal course. For the New Testament asserts that God took a dead body and changed it from a decaying one to one that could never decay again. And thus the New Testament understands God's action here to be somewhat like other causes in the world, and so it is strictly mythological in Bultmann's terms.

Bultmann puts these four different types of material in the one category of myth and treats them all the same. This should not be done because they are not all the same kind of material. Only the fourth category, Supernatural Actions, really opposes what Bultmann calls the modern, scientific understanding of the world. The New Testament says that Bultmann is wrong in thinking that God never acts in the events of history in a visible manner, for the New Testament proclaims that in fact God has so acted in the resurrection of Christ. The question that now must be raised is whether or not Bultmann is right in accepting the assumptions of the scientific method as his absolute and final authority.

THE ASSUMPTION OF A SCIENTIFIC WORLD VIEW

One charge against Bultmann is that Liberalism, which he depends on, is out of date. It is said that his understanding of the scientific world view is a century old. Many believed then that science had shown that the world was a closed universe in which no divine forces could intervene. Now it is realized that science has not demonstrated this, but merely assumes it as part of its method for dealing with the observable world. Its working assumption is that there will be no transcendent, supernatural causes acting. But this is only an assumption. It is not a scientific conclusion, any more than the assumption that it is better to do good than to do evil is a scientific conclusion.

Scientists in the twentieth century have been less presumptive than their forebears. They have come to realize that they do not write unbreakable natural laws. They instead observe what they have seen *so far* and express their observations as natural laws. It is recognized that there will be a great many new facts revealed in the future that will change their present conclusions. Scientists still assume that there are no forces other than observable, measurable forces that they need consider. There is no other way they can go about their business of understanding and observing the natural world.

Their results, however, are always only approximately true. For example, Newton's laws of motion have been superseded by Einstein's Principle of Relativity. Newton's laws are so close to being true, however, especially for normal life, and are so useful because of their simplicity, that they are used and taught as valid. Likewise the assumption that only natural causes will be met by the scientist is so useful an assumption, and so close to being true, that it is a valid foundation for the scientific method.

But when this working assumption is made an absolute, philosophical assertion of unconditional validity, then it has gone beyond the bounds of its proven usefulness. It has become a statement of faith which has no more scientific validity than the Christian statement of faith that God has acted in history. It is in fact a statement of unfaith, comparable to the views "life is meaningless," or "death is the final goal for mankind."

Will we adopt the philosophical faith that God cannot intervene in the course of events in the world? Or will we take the position of the Bible which says that God has so intervened and continues to do so? If we adopt the biblical view, this does not mean that we must accept every report of a supposedly divine intervention in history. We can still discriminate between those stories that are well attested historically (e.g. the resurrection of Jesus) and those that are probably mythological expressions of the writer's faith (e.g. the rising of many dead men at the time of the death of Jesus, Matt. 27:52f.).

THE IMPORTANCE OF GOD'S EMPIRICAL ACTS

Bultmann believes that God does not intervene in the natural course of events, but acts only within the existential sphere. As part of his argument he says that even if God did act in the natural course of events this would say nothing at all about His relationship to man in the existential sphere: forgiveness of sins, release from anxiety and despair, hope in God's ultimate victory over evil. Bultmann says there is no connection between the two spheres as far as God's acting is concerned, as in some church members' lives there is unfortunately no connection between the religious sphere of Sunday worship and the secular sphere of life in the office.

The Bible denies this. It says that God acts in the natural course of events, healing people from sickness, rescuing them from danger, and judging them by bringing punishment upon them. It says that God's actions in the empirical, observable sphere are connected with His actions in the existential sphere, within man.

To a large extent these acts of God are means for demonstrating (though not proving) the truth of His action within man. God can be the (spiritual) Protector and God of Israel, and deserves to be, because He has already proven Himself in the (physical) Exodus from Egypt; Jesus proclaims His (spiritual) authority to forgive sins by (physically) healing a man (Mark 2:10f); Jesus is shown to be "Son of God in power" by the resurrection (Rom. 1:4). A man who dives into a rushing river to rescue his son draws his son into a deeper personal relationship by that act than he would have had if the rescue had not been necessary. A physical event often has important spiritual results.

Bultmann thinks that this attempted attestation of God's spiritual meaning for our lives by reference to a physical event was a mistake. He believes that when the eternal meaning of the Cross is thought to be demonstrated by the resurrection, then faith is denied. For him faith means believing in the Cross even though there is no evidence to support such a faith. Simply because the disciples believed and began the preaching that has come down to us, we are called on by Bultmann to make a leap of faith and believe in the Cross as they did.

Many critics of Bultmann claim that this is his weakest point, for they say he is asking for a blind faith that has even less support than the Church's claim that God has acted in the events of history. Bultmann believes that faith can only be faith if it is understood as totally separated from knowledge that would give it a foundation. His critics say that without some knowledge as a foundation there is no reason at all for them to believe that the Cross of Christ is the act of God for the salvation of mankind. Rather than making the gospel acceptable to modern man, who demands evidence to support assertions, they say Bultmann has made the gospel impossible to accept. Thousands of other men were crucified by the Romans. Why should we believe in Christ rather than in the thief on the other cross who died with him? Why should we accept the disciples' faith?

Bultmann will not even allow the Gospels' description of Jesus' life and teaching to be used as foundation for faith in the Cross. He thinks there is very little in the Gospels that can be accepted as historically accurate, so we cannot even use Jesus' claims about Himself and the meaning of His death as the basis for our faith. We are simply confronted by the gospel message and told: believe in the Cross of Christ as the act of God for your salvation. When we ask, "Why should I?" Bultmann's answer is, "Because this is the Word of God, and you are not to question it."

THE CENTRALITY OF THE RESURRECTION

The most important objection of all is this: If Bultmann denies the reality of the resurrection, must he not conclude that the Church was founded on an error? The Church proclaimed that Jesus had been raised from the dead. It proclaimed that this was the heart of its faith, so that without the resurrection there would be no gospel and no Church. If there was no resurrection, Paul said, men would not have been saved from their sins, but would still be as miserable as they had been before Jesus came. Bultmann says that Jesus was not raised. He says that the only "resurrection" was the rise of the Easter faith of the disciples, their coming to believe that Jesus' death was the event of God's salvation. But if the disciples were wrong, if they believed God had raised Jesus from the dead when in fact He had not done so, is not the Church then based upon a mistake so that it ought to close its doors?

Rampant Skepticism

Since Bultmann agrees that the Church ought not close its doors, it is likely that he is far too radical in his skepticism about the historical value of the recorded life of Jesus. In his theology all that Bultmann needs to know about Jesus was that He lived and that He died on a cross. Everything else in the Gospels is, according to him, the theology of the early Church and not an historical report. We have seen in a previous chapter, however, that there is a substantial amount of evidence to support the Church's proclamation of the resurrection.

The amount and variety of evidence cannot merely be cast

aside as Bultmann does, if we wish to think in a logical, historical, even scientific manner. A scientist does not start out knowing what is possible and impossible, for there is always new evidence confronting him which he never expected. The theologian must act the same way with the resurrection, taking the evidence seriously, rather than just discarding it because "modern man finds it impossible to believe in resurrections."

Can the faith of the Church stand, if with Bultmann we deny that the resurrection happened? There are theologians who deny that it happened in a physical sense: that is, they deny that the body of Jesus was raised. But they claim that Jesus Himself, His "spirit," was raised. They claim that He is alive and has conquered death in the same way that we, as Christians will be alive and will conquer death because of Him. But Bultmann appears to deny that there was any resurrection at all. For him the New Testament message of the resurrection was simply a means of expressing the truth that God had saved man through the Cross of Christ. For many Christians today, however, belief in the risen Christ who is alive and present, acting in the world today, is a central part of their faith. This Bultmann denies by discarding the resurrection as an historical event.

Ambiguous Faith

If the Church is right in believing that Christ is the present Lord of the Church, then Bultmann has gone too far when he denies that Christ was raised from the dead. He tries to hedge a little by saying that Christ meets us in the preaching of the gospel, but it is not certain what he means by this. Probably he means that in the preaching of the Church we are confronted by the meaning of Christ, as we are confronted by the meaning of Lincoln when we read the Gettysburg address or hear a political speaker invoke his name and story. Lincoln is dead, however, but the Church believes that Christ is alive, an assertion that is virtually impossible if the resurrection is denied.

The truth of the resurrection faith, however, is not tied to belief in a specific mode of resurrection. Christ is the Risen Lord of the Church today in an invisible, spiritual manner. Thus the Church's faith is not irrevocably tied to the apostles' belief that Christ's body was raised. Even if His body had been raised so that a neutral, scientific witness could have sworn to it, this would not prove the Church's faith, for Lazarus was raised but died again.

The ambiguous descriptions of Christ's appearances indicate that the resurrection could well have been an event in which God acted secretly, raising Christ Himself to a new form of life. Whether or not this distinction between a physical and a spiritual resurrection is valid, it is fairly certain that Bultmann is wrong in thinking that he can deny the resurrection completely but still affirm the validity of the Church.

CONCLUSION

Bultmann's day as the center of theological controversy has come and gone. But the questions he raised are still the central questions for theology, even though his answers to them are not widely accepted. His desire to make the gospel understandable and meaningful to man today is the desire of every Christian. The distinction he made between the existential side of life and the empirical side is a distinction that is of central importance for understanding modern theology. The question that he raised of how we are to understand God's action in history is still the central question of biblical interpretation. Whatever conclusions are drawn about Bultmann's own answers, all who are interested in Christian understanding are in his debt.

9

Biblical Interpretation Today

The final answers are not yet in. Every generation adds new insight to the never-ending quest of understanding the Bible. The insights of the past must be used as building blocks that enable children to climb higher than their fathers. The climb continues, but participants face two primary requirements: they must know what their fathers have said, to build on their insight and learn from their mistakes; they must be open to the future, willing to question anything which seems to obstruct deeper understanding.

The nineteenth century emphasis on the Bible as Literature and History led to the reaction of Barth and Biblical Theology after World War I. The objectivity and "primitive" nature of that way of thinking led to Bultmann's demythologizing and quest for subjective relevance after World War II. Now, a generation of Cold War has led theologians beyond Bultmann, to the questions that he raised but did not answer satisfactorily.

Present-day biblical interpreters have taken up issues that Bultmann de-emphasized. The first is the problem of the Historical Jesus. This had been shelved for fifty years, since Barth drew biblical studies away from history to theology. The second is the problem of the Future, which plays a large part in biblical thought. But Bultmann's theology virtually ignored it by emphasizing the necessity for decision in the present.

THE PROBLEM OF THE HISTORICAL JESUS

FAITH AND THE HISTORIAN

For the first seventeen hundred years of the Church's life there was general satisfaction with the word portrait of Jesus given in the four Gospels. Christians believed that the Gospels were accurate, and complete enough for men to know Jesus as He really was. Basically the Church looked on the Gospels as eye-witness reports by reporters who were primarily interested in the accuracy of their story.

Then in 1778 a German Christian, Hermann Reimarus, suggested that the Gospel reports were not the same as newspaper stories but were closer to historical novels. Non-Christians had rejected the accuracy of the New Testament before, but Reimarus spoke from within the Church and so was much more widely listened to. If today a Russian politician declares that the United States is decaying politically and socially, it is seen as propaganda and ignored. But when an American politician or historian says the same thing, it will be heard and pondered seriously. So was Reimarus' thought.

Pandora's Box

Reimarus opened a Pandora's Box of historical problems by trying to decide which parts of the Gospel portrait of Jesus are historically accurate and which are not. The goal was to assemble the accurate evidence into a new picture, known as "The Historical Jesus," though it could better be called, "The historian's Jesus."

First, John's Gospel was recognized as differing radically from the three Synoptic Gospels. It was concluded that the Synoptics are closer to Jesus as He really was, for John gave the appearance of literary artistry. The second step was the observation that Paul and John speak of Jesus as "Christ," "Lord," and "God," titles that the Jesus of the Synoptics never used

of Himself. This led to the conclusion that all the exalted
language used of Jesus, and all the supernatural traits found
in the Gospel story were Church additions to the original
story of "a simple Jewish rabbi."

These two conclusions were reached by about 1850, and
for the next fifty years, hundreds of books poured off the
presses, each presenting "the historical Jesus." The authors
eliminated anything in the Gospels that appeared "primitive"
or did not appeal to nineteenth century man. Then each
author used his imagination to create historical connections
and psychological justifications that would allow him to write
a full-length biography. Calling the Gospels historical novels
and so unreliable, these "historians" turned out a warehouse
full of modern historical novels.

The End of the Old Quest

This glut of books halted in 1906 when Albert Schweitzer
wrote his epoch-making account, *The Quest of the Historical
Jesus.* Schweitzer showed that each nineteenth century author
had created an historical Jesus in his own image. One man
described Him as a socialist revolutionary, another as a capital-
ist salesman, a third as a pastoral dreamer. None of the books
really presented Jesus of Nazareth, however, for all of them
ignored (as did previous centuries) the heart of His preaching
— the imminent eruption of the Kingdom of God. The nineteenth century "Lives of Jesus" were like a biography of Lincoln that could be written today ignoring slavery because it
has disappeared. Without that issue a "Life of Lincoln" is a
hollow shell. So were the "Liberal Lives of Jesus."

Further study in the twentieth century has convinced most
scholars that the failures chronicled by Schweitzer were inevitable. No full-length biography of Jesus can ever be written
because the Gospels do not provide adequate information.
They are not primarily historical sources, but proclamations

of the Church's faith. They do not give chronological or psychological information, for they put stories and sayings together in topical order, not showing the historical connections between events.

Some scholars, notably Barth and Bultmann, go even further, asserting that the attempt to write an accurate biography of Jesus is not only impossible, but is unnecessary and even sinful. To Bultmann the quest is unnecessary, because all that men need to know of Jesus is that He lived and died. The quest is sinful because it is an attempt to "prove" the gospel.

The Liberals of the nineteenth century had thought that an accurate portrait of Jesus would convince all men of the logic of following Him. But Barth and Bultmann knew that following Him comes only as a leap of faith that cannot be proven. Trying to find proof is evidence of a refusal to believe. It would be the same as a girl researching a young man's background to see how truthful others thought he was and how he had treated all other girls, before she responded to his "I love you."

THE NECESSITY FOR A NEW QUEST

The skepticism of Barth and Bultmann drove scholars away from the problem of the historical Jesus for many years. But in 1954 the debate was reopened by some of Bultmann's pupils who felt he had gone too far. This was not a return to the Old Quest, an attempt to write a full biography of Jesus. Rather it was a more modest "New" Quest, avoiding most of the pitfalls of the old.

The object of the New Quest is to determine the connection between the "Historical Jesus" and the "Christ of faith." The historical Jesus is the portrait of Jesus that can be sketched by a skeptical historian. It consists of the most certain facts and sayings in the Gospels, those that no one can reasonably doubt. The Christ of faith is the Risen Lord who is experienced today and worshiped as God in the Church universal.

Requirement for Faith?

Bultmann's former pupils say that if there is no real connection between Jesus as He really was and the message that the Church preaches about Him, then the Church is preaching superstition. They believe that if Jesus denied that He was of any importance for mankind then it would be hard to accept the Church's message that He is the Savior of mankind. If it could be shown that He was a coward who used every trick in the book to escape the Cross, then it would be hard "to accept joyfully the Cross of Christ," which Bultmann calls us to bear.

If the Church ignores historical study of the traditions about Jesus, it is in danger of worshiping a mere man, of basing its life on a set of myths. Avoiding such study would be like a historian of medieval England assuming that since Shakespeare used ancient chronicles in his plays, his characters and plots are true to history. As the historian must get behind Shakespeare, so the Church must get behind the Gospels.

The New Questers say the Church must do this to be certain about its foundation. But it must also undertake the quest to avoid leaving it to non-Christians whose objections to the gospel will color their accounts. When a politician makes an ambiguous statement that is distorted by his opponents, his press secretary must present his real meaning in order not to leave an erroneous impression before the public. So too the Church must undertake historical study of Jesus.

Answering Objections

Scholars generally agree that preventing distortions by opponents is valid and makes the New Quest a relative necessity. Many claim, however, that seeking certainty about the Church's foundation is the old Liberal search for sinful security that Barth and Bultmann denounced fifty years ago. And yet it is not really a search for security, for the "New Questers" know that the truth of the gospel cannot be demonstrated. But some objections to believing in Christ that have been raised by historians can be eliminated. In this task, scholars are acting like a man who defends himself against gossip that his wife has heard about him. He knows that he cannot prove to his wife that she ought to love and trust him, but he can show that the specific objections she has raised are not true enough to force her to distrust him.

Some historians in the nineteenth century claimed that Jesus never lived, but was the mythical hero of a Greek cult, like Dionysius or other Greek gods. Another objection was that Jesus was only a Jewish teacher of ethics whom the Church misunderstood to be Savior and Lord. Answering these objections, especially the latter, is the heart of the task of the New Quest. This answer makes it possible for a non-Christian to be confronted by the gospel as a moral question: "Am I willing to confess my sin, receive God's judgment and forgiveness, and commit my life to Jesus' cause?" The New Quest does not answer this question for us. It clears the air so the question can be heard and not avoided by intellectual objections.

In a similar way the cause of Civil Rights today is a moral question, one of commitment. But intellectual objections are raised: "Blacks are already equal"; "They are lazy, wanting something for nothing"; "Other people's rights are being abused." These objections can and must be answered. But even when a man hears the answers, he may still be unwilling to commit himself to the cause. The New Questers are supplying answers, but only God can promote commitment.

NEW POSSIBILITY

Once it has been granted that historical discussion of Jesus' life, work, and self-understanding are important to the Church,

the next question is whether the New Quest is possible. The
Old Quest turned out to be impossible because there were no
adequate materials to provide a full length biography of Jesus.
Each biographer made up his own connecting links and psychological details. The New Quest is much more modest because it does not attempt a full scale biography of Jesus. Instead of seeking to portray the events of Jesus' life, it is seeking
Jesus' own self-understanding, in order to see whether He
thought of Himself in the way the Church thinks of Him.

Skeptical Method

But can we know what Jesus really thought of Himself?
Most Christians would say, "Certainly, we go to the Gospels
and look up the sayings of Jesus concerning Himself, especially those speaking of the Son of Man, of which there are
many." But these former pupils of Bultmann's who are the
chief advocates of the New Quest, all agree that a historian
cannot use any material in the Gospels that directly reflects
the early Church's faith in Jesus. The early Church thought
of Him as the Son of Man. Therefore, these scholars say, it
may well have been the early Church which put these sayings
and even the title, "Son of Man," on Jesus' lips. So these scholars bypass all the clear statements of what Jesus thought of
Himself, going instead to His more ambiguous sayings, which
do not directly express the Church's faith.

This procedure is very similar to that used by a detective
in questioning a suspect. The direct assertions the suspect
makes are likely to be for his own benefit and protection. They
are not the detective's primary interest, for he knows they
could well be propaganda. Instead, he listens for hints in the
way the suspect says things, extra details that are not important
in his main assertions. These extras are usually included unconsciously, and are likely to be true. Thus the detective
counts on them, and builds his questioning and his case on
them. In the same way the historian puts to one side the

Gospel statements that are direct assertions of the Church's faith, for they could be propaganda. He looks for clues in details, words, and sayings that are not prominent. Neither the detective nor the historian can claim to know that the direct assertions are false, but it is a good possibility and so they do not depend on them.

Inadequate Results

By this means the New Questers hope to show that Jesus appears as a unique figure who can be the basis for the Christian Church, even when the most skeptical historical screening of the evidence is allowed. They have presented a variety of characteristics as central to the historical Jesus. One says that the important thing about Him was His "authority," the way He spoke for God; another says it was His "freedom," that He did not let religious and other outdated myths constrain Him; another says that it is the "faith of Jesus" that is central.

These varied "central" characteristics are not mutually exclusive. Nevertheless, even the combination of all three does not demonstrate any intrinsic connection between the Jesus of history and the Christ of faith. Certainly, "authority" and "freedom" are attributes of both the historical Jesus and the Risen Christ, but this is not enough, anymore than there is enough evidence to arrest a man on suspicion of murder because he and the murderer are both white, with black hair, and about six feet tall.

Even if half a dozen more common attributes could be presented, they would not overcome the fact that the historical Jesus was a Jewish rabbi who worshiped and prayed to the one God of Israel, and the Christ of faith is worshiped as God. That gap cannot be fully crossed no matter how many common characteristics of the two are presented. The New Quest has succeeded in pointing to the common characteristics, but has failed in its task because it ignores the only possible link between the earthly Jesus and the present Lord of the Church.

SAME OLD PROBLEM

The central clue to the connection between the historical Jesus and the Christ of faith is not in Jesus' words and deeds but in an event the New Questers discount — the resurrection. They have largely accepted Bultmann's philosophical view that God does not act in the physical world, and so they deny that the resurrection could have happened. Only when one denies this central message of the New Testament does the problem of how "Jesus the preacher" became the "Christ who was preached" arise. The resurrection provides the link between them.

The Missing Link

One of Bultmann's pupils, Günther Bornkamm, has called Bultmann's denial of the fact of the resurrection "disastrous." Bultmann asserted that the resurrection happened only within the disciples as they believed that Jesus' death was God's great act. Bornkamm disagrees. To interpret the resurrection in this way would be to turn all the New Testament stories of the resurrection upside down, for they say it was Jesus Himself who was raised. The disciples doubted this, even after hearing the good news, and only gradually did the presence of Christ with them convince them that He was really risen. Bornkamm, in his book on Jesus, does not go into detail about his belief in the resurrection, but somehow he wishes to assert that it is an historical event, something that really happened to Jesus.

The difference between Bultmann and Bornkamm over the resurrection is like the difference between two preachers who came to a concentration camp in Germany a week apart in May of 1945. The first said to the people, "Believe that the war is over; act as if it were, and you will be free within yourself." The second said simply, "The war *is* over. You *are* free." This second message is the heart of the New Testament resurrection faith which Bornkamm guardedly affirms.

Vindication

The resurrection of Jesus meant to His disciples that the central part of His message had been vindicated. He had asserted that the Kingdom of God was about to break in upon man, and one aspect of the Kingdom was the resurrection of believers. Jesus' own resurrection was the first step on the way to the resurrection of all, the beginning of the End of the World. God has finally broken in upon the world, pointing to the future when He will bring His Kingdom to fulfillment. Thus Jesus' proclamation of the imminence of the Kingdom was fulfilled in His own resurrection.

Denying the resurrection brings with it two conclusions: that the early Church's central message — "He is Risen" — was wrong! Jesus' central message — "The Kingdom is at hand" — was a mistake. These two are inseparable, so there is no chance of denying the Church's faith in the Risen Christ and getting back to "the simple gospel of Jesus." Trying to continue to be the Church while denying the resurrection is pulling the foundation out from under the entire structure. It is as foolish as getting married without a desire and commitment to "love, honor and cherish."

There has been a rising chorus of objections to Bultmann's view, which was typical of the nineteenth century, that resurrections are impossible because we don't see them happening today. Many now realize that if we are to learn anything from history we must be willing to let history speak for itself even if it means asserting the unexpected. The resurrection is the chief example of learning something new from history. If the evidence is adequate, we should be willing to allow our understanding of ourselves and our world to be challenged by it. If not, then our unbelief has no authority for the Christian who knows that there is more to life than science or historical study can discover.

THE FUTURE: THE GOD OF PROMISE

THE OLD AND THE NEW

The resurrection, then, is the missing link in a true understanding of Jesus and the Church. It is also central to the second important post-Bultmannian emphasis — the Future. Barth and Bultmann in their concern to stress the relevance of the biblical message to the present life of man, played down the aspect of the future. In this they adopted one of the short-sighted characteristics of their Liberal teachers.

The Lost Future

During the last century, when the "Liberal Lives of Jesus" were being written, the biblical emphasis upon the future was greatly played down. At the turn of the century, however, Albert Schweitzer pointed out that if we ignore the concept of the future coming of the Kingdom of God, we completely misunderstand Jesus. He was greatly concerned about the future. Most modern expositions of the teaching of Jesus realize this. But it has not been taken as seriously by those who try to present the Bible's relevance for man today.

Bultmann is the best example of this tendency to de-emphasize the future aspect of Christian faith. He believed that concentration upon the future, the End of the World, was a characteristic that Jesus and the early Christians had taken over from the Jews of their time. Therefore, said Bultmann, it was merely part of the Jewish language and understanding that Jesus adopted in order to bring His message to the Jews.

In fact, Bultmann claims the New Testament shows in its later writings that the future was played down almost completely. He points for evidence to the Gospel of John, which speaks of "eternal life" as something possessed by believers now, not a gift that awaits them in the future. In order to prove that John is concerned only with the present, Bultmann has to eliminate many future references to "the last day" (John 6:39, 54, etc.), as if they were clumps of crabgrass in the otherwise perfect lawn of John's Gospel. He claims that they are interpolations by a later editor and not part of the original writing. But there is no evidence to support him, other than his own conclusions about John's "real meaning."

The real source of Bultmann's objection to Christianity's concern with the future is his existentialist philosophy. From that philosophy Bultmann adopts the viewpoint that only the present matters, for "the meaning of history lies always in the present." By holding to such a belief Bultmann almost entirely ignores the determinative nature of the future in biblical thought.

As his Liberal teachers had concentrated entirely on how a man lives now, so Bultmann stressed that what matters is whether a man decides *now* for or against Christ. In this emphasis, Bultmann was like the man who lives his life only from day to day, never planning for next week, or setting a goal for his life.

The Future Regained

Continuing Bultmann's program of interpreting the Bible only in terms of today has faced scholars with two obstacles. In the first place man is naturally futuristic, so his concern about the future cannot be suppressed as Bultmann seems to desire. "Hope springs eternal in the human breast." Any Christian theology that does not concern itself with hope will not be fully relevant and will leave the way open for non-Christian hopes. Secondly, it is impossible to read the Bible and not be overwhelmed by its concentration on the Future. If we ignore that concentration we are misinterpreting its meaning.

These two essential obstacles to Bultmann's method of interpretation have been most explosively probed by Jürgen Moltmann, a young German theologian, in his epoch-making book, *The Theology of Hope*. In this book he expresses a new trend in theological thinking — that our God is a God of Promise, and man is a creature of hope.

The Church's silence on hope for the world left the way open for Marx to place all his eggs in that basket. He pointed forward to his dream of the equality of all men in a classless society, and thereby he commanded the imagination of millions. The Church in Europe today is talking with Marxists, for Christians have learned that the Marxist emphasis on hope is a part of the Christian heritage.

Every man lives by hope, for the choices he makes now reflect where he hopes to go. If he sees the ultimate goal as being rich, he will make decisions whose primary aim is to increase his wealth. If he hopes for a classless society, he will take steps to promote that. If he hopes for a world in which all men are reconciled to God and each other, he will try to move towards that goal. Man is a creature of hope. The only question is: what does he hope for?

GOD'S PROMISES IN THE BIBLE

The God who created this creature of hope is a God of promise. According to Moltmann, the biblical witness characterizes God most often as going somewhere and drawing His people with Him. He is not a static God. He is a God of Hope and History, promising to send His people on, and then fulfilling those promises.

The Pilgrim People

In the Old Testament, God revealed Himself to Israel consistently in the form of Promise. He made Himself known to Abraham in His promise to make a great nation of his descendants. He made Himself known to Moses in His promise to rescue Israel from Egypt. He made Himself known to David in His promise to make his family the rulers of Israel forever. Israel's God was the God of a nomadic tribe that moved from place to place, from experience to experience, always finding something new. And in this way, Israel came to believe in God as a God of history, One who was going somewhere, doing something new.

When Israel settled down in Canaan, they were attracted to the static nature gods of the land. But they were not seduced, for their God was very different; He was moving onward. The difference between worshiping a nature god and worshiping the God of History is the difference between night and day. Nature worshipers believed that there was nothing new in the world, that the cyclical birth and death of nature each year were the ultimate realities to which man had to conform. Man was caught by the fateful turn of Nature, ground down from year to year like the slave in a salt mine.

God's promises to Israel created an entirely new outlook on life. Israel began to believe that there is change and growth possible in the future, for the framework of life is not nature, but the outworking of the unique promises of God. Israel learned that man is not trapped by Nature, but is free to respond to God and take part in the future possibilities He has promised. Instead of being a slave in a salt mine he is the architect, constructor, and achiever of civilization. The difference is the outgrowth of an experience of the God of Promise.

The experience was not like that of a child who is promised ice cream and then settles down comfortably after receiving it, for God's promises always lead on to the future, for every fulfillment contains a new promise. The promises of Land, Kingship, and Return from Exile were fulfilled. Yet God kept His people unsatisfied, for He pointed them forward to a Great Day, when He would send a second David to bring all Israel's hopes to fruition.

End and Beginning

In the New Testament, Israel's hope for God's Messiah was fulfilled in Jesus. He was a son of David. He was the king of Israel. He did bring salvation to His people. His appearance was the beginning of the End of the World. In these and many more ways Jesus fulfilled the promises of God in the Old Testament. One of the most important of all the titles given to Jesus in the New Testament is "Fulfillment of God's Promises."

But it was striking that Jesus almost never appeared to be exactly the fulfillment that Israel had hoped for. The new Davidic king they had expected was to be a warrior to overthrow their oppressors. The salvation they longed for was political and religious independence. The End of the World they anticipated was a transformed earth where God would reign with Israel as His regent. The fulfillment that came in Jesus raised as many questions as it answered, and so most Jews refused to believe that He was truly God's answer to their hopes.

They had hoped for political freedom and so rejected God's gift of Himself by which they could receive freedom from the evil that enslaved them from within their minds and hearts. They were like a child who wants a comic book subscription for Christmas and then gets upset when his parents give him an encyclopedia instead. They would not let God be His gracious Self by giving far more than they ever had hoped for.

Jesus' life, death, and resurrection were the beginning of the total fulfillment of God's promises and man's hopes. But only the beginning. Death, sin, and corrupt institutions remained. God pointed His people to the promised kingdom, when all men would live together, reconciled to God and each other, when all the evil of this world would be ended.

THE FOUNDATION OF THE FUTURE

The Bible's future concern does not depend on human

ideas or revelations of what might come. Instead, the hope of mankind is built on present experience of the God of Hope, and knowledge that He has faithfully fulfilled His promises in the past. This is exactly the same kind of foundation that all hope is built on. A child's hope for good from his father in the future is based on his relationship to his father in the present, and the memory of the good gifts he has given in the past.

Historical Hope

The chief event in Israel's past was the Exodus, God's rescue of His people from slavery in Egypt. From that they learned what God is like, what His aims in the world are, and so what His people can expect from Him as fulfilled promises in the future. In a similar way the people of America found their future laid out before them in the first one hundred days of Franklin Roosevelt's presidency. They learned where his sympathies lay, what kind of action he dared and determined to take, and so they had a foretaste of the next eight years.

In the Exodus, Israel learned that God remembers promises, the promises made to Abraham — to be his God and to give his descendants the land of Canaan. The first fulfilled promise gave Israel the foundation upon which their hopes could be built in the future. They knew, as subsequent ages learned, that they worshiped a faithful God, One who was willing and able to carry out the promises He had made.

Conquering Evil Today

That fulfilled promise of the Exodus provides the certainty and direction for Christian hope today. We worship the God of the Exodus (who is also the God known to us through many other similar events) and experience today His love and concern for His people. Therefore, on the basis of that past event and our present experience, we have a secure hope in the way He will show Himself to us in the future. As the Supreme

Court showed itself to be an advocate of racial equality in 1954, and in 1969 said "equality now," so we have a secure hope that as long as it remains the same Court it will be a bulwark of equality.

There is one difference between Israel's hope after the Exodus, and Christian hope today — the extent of God's care. Israel believed that only their nation was the object of God's love, but God's action in Christ made it clear that the whole world is the arena of His active concern. The hope that we have in the God of the Exodus is a hope that the whole world will be led out of slavery into the freedom and fulfillment of a Promised Land. In a similar way, the vision of Americans has expanded greatly in this generation, so that we know we are not fully free unless our brothers in Mississippi and Mali are also free.

This hope, for a Promised Land for all men, which has been generated within us by God's loving presence, is the basis for our involvement in God's world. He has promised a world in which all men are free, at peace, and fulfilled as human beings. The meaning of life, we now can see, is climbing on His bandwagon, working to achieve His ends. We believe that wherever there is slavery, He is at work opposing it, be it the slavery of poverty and racism in American ghettos, the tyranny of dictatorship in China or South America, the slavery of illiteracy and disease the world over. As politicians sit on the fence only until they see the way the political wind is blowing, so Christians have seen that the wave of the Future is God's conquest of personal and institutional evil. Once we have felt the wind, we cannot sit on the fence any longer.

THE RESURRECTION VICTORY

While the historical fulfillments of God's promises are very important to the hope of His people, still they must take second place to the hope of eternal life that is given in the resurrection of Jesus. The two hopes need to be distinguished, but they must not be divided. The goal of a just and peaceful world is a different hope than the promise of eternal life. Yet in their difference they are intimately tied together in several ways.

Time and Eternity

The Guarantor of both goals is the same God of Promise, so they fit together intimately in His good intentions for man. But an even more important connection is that our hope for a transformed earth depends on the victory of the resurrection. That is paradoxical, for we would expect the dependence to be the other way around: the easier, more natural hope of a better world would be the foundation for the hope of resurrection and eternal life — hopes that are beyond our natural comprehensions and expectations. Because a child has received a bicycle from his father, he then can hope to receive a car when he gets older. Our vision is more easily directed to circumstances closest to us.

But the God we worship reverses this order: because He has given Himself to us in Jesus Christ, therefore there is nothing that He will hold back that is good for us. Our problem is that we have difficulty hoping for a bicycle (a transformed earth) and so God has given us the guarantee of a car (eternal life) first. Because we have the security and certainty of the greater gift, we can give ourselves fully to the task of working with Him to achieve the lesser.

The Greatest Hope

We need the great promise of resurrection because of the great threat of meaninglessness — death. The meaning of a journey is found in its destination, and so the meaning of life depends on where it is heading. If the end result of all my love and commitment is that my loved ones and I return to dust, then the goal has not been worth the effort. If the end result of all the blood, sweat, and tears of man throughout the earth's history is going to be the incineration of this planet in a collision with the sun, then the whole process has been meaningless.

If we think that life is meaningless because its goal is dust, then we cannot really give ourselves to making men and society better before they turn to dust. If we are to adopt God's goal of a transformed earth, it can only be because we know that all will not simply be obliterated. We can only give ourselves completely to God's hopes if we believe that in losing our earthly lives we are not losing anything of eternal value. I can lay down my life for my friend if I can believe that in doing so I am truly being myself, and not eternally destroying myself.

Thus the New Testament emphasis upon resurrection and eternal life is not an other-worldly, irrelevant addition to a reasonable guide to life. The hope of eternal life is the bedrock upon which Christian life is built, just as every way of life is built on an expectation of what the future holds. The Future is an absolutely essential aspect of Christian thought, as much as the Present and the Past. All three are united in our eternal God.

Here We Stand

The only basis we have for our hope of eternal life, our hope that sacrifice and love in this life have meaning, is the resurrection of Jesus. Without His resurrection, evil would have triumphed in the crucifixion. If He was not raised, then the love that He lived is not the deepest reality in the world. If God did not raise Him, then He ended His existence with a cry of god-forsakenness on His lips. If Christ is still dead, then He cannot be the living Lord of the Church, and His assertion that God's reign over evil began in Himself is false. Without the resurrection Jesus appears as helpless and as foolish as King

Canute standing at the seashore and ordering the waves to recede.

So there is no getting around the New Testament witness to the resurrection. It is not an optional addition to the Christian faith. It is its very heart. If we ignore the New Testament's central assertion — that Christ is risen — then we misinterpret the gospel message. We have something else entirely. The Christian message without the resurrection is a book without pictures or words: it may look like a book from the outside, but inside it is only the sham of blank pages.

The absolute importance of Jesus' resurrection is not simply that it describes Him. Rather it says something about God and about History, for it was the first fulfillment of God's ancient promise of the end of death. Easter was not just the reversal of the injustice of Good Friday. It was the beginning of the reversal of all injustice. It does not mark the end of only Jesus' god-forsakenness, but is a foretaste of the end of all estrangement between God and man. It is not just the release of one man from death, but it is the victory of God over Death itself, Mankind's release from the slavery of death. In Christ we find that Death does not have the final word — God has it. He is the Alpha and the Omega, the Beginning *and* the End.

CONCLUSION

We cannot know which direction the interpretation of the Bible will take next. The lessons of this century have not been lost, for each generation adds to the solid foundation of biblical understanding that has been laid by their fathers. The biblical theologians showed clearly that the Bible is concerned mainly about God's actions in history for man's salvation. Bultmann showed that there is a problem of understanding how God acts, for the Bible speaks symbolically and mythically in a way that modern man often does not readily comprehend.

Following Bultmann's emphasis on the need to speak the language of modern man, two new emphases have emerged. The first is how the man Jesus could be also the Lord of the Church. The solution is found in the resurrection. That solution is part and parcel of the other new emphasis of post-Bultmann theology — the Future. Only by understanding God's promises and goals can we live a Christian life, for only then do we really know who God is.

In the next decade other new points of departure will be suggested, for none of these discussed so far is fully adequate. Every approach has its limitations. Biblical scholars are like the blind men who come across an elephant and give differing descriptions of what it is. Gradually they learn from each other and reach a more comprehensive view. But they are still blind, and none can offer a complete and final description.

The task is exciting, however, for there are always new discoveries ahead, and the truth that has already been presented needs to be integrated. We must combine history, literature, and theology to unite the past, present, and future so that the whole truth, not just parts of it, will belong to all who wish to understand the Bible.

Other books by Peter W. Macky—

The Pursuit of the Divine Snowman. A beginning search for modern symbols that takes up the central characteristics of the biblical witness to God and tries to express them in modern language. New stories, new images, new experiences and events help the modern reader see how his own experience is tied into the biblical picture of God. #80484.

Violence: Right or Wrong. Shows that to understand violence requires the insights of a variety of disciplines. A close look at biological, psychological, sociological, historical, and biblical materials leads the Christian to ask: What is my role to be? The answer, Dr. Macky points out, lies in implementing Christ's teachings in one's personal situation. #80309.

A series of special interest, Makers of the Modern Theological Mind, edited by Bob E. Patterson

Karl Barth, by David Mueller. A look at one of the deepest thinkers, finest lecturers and most prolific writers in contemporary Christianity, often called "father of the modern church." #80254.

Dietrich Bonhoeffer, by Dallas M. Roark. An introduction to the brilliant young theologian executed by the Nazis when he was only 39. Gives a brief review of his life and insights into his major writings. #80253.

Rudolf Bultmann, by Morris Ashcraft. A study of the man who sought to answer the question "How can modern scientific man understand the strange religious language of the Bible?" Considers Bultmann's views on the relationship of faith and existence and demythologizing. #80252.

Emil Brunner, by J. Edward Humphrey. About one of the great system-builders of 20th century Christian theology and his understandings of the doctrines of God, man, Christ, the church, faith, eternal hope. Helpful explanations of his key concepts: divine self-communication, personhood, truth as encounter, etc. #80453.

Teilhard de Chardin, by Doran McCarty. An incisive examination of Teilhard's thought: the nature of God, the phenomenon of man, the structure of reality, creation and evolution, democracy and totalitarianism; explanations of Teilhard's unique terminology: centreism, withinness, Christogenesis, noosphere, the Omega Point. #80436.

Charles Hartshorne, by Alan Gragg. A study of one of the most eminent living philosophers, analyzing why his philosophical and theological positions must be regarded as a fresh, creative approach to traditional theological issues, and why his positions are powerful influences in contemporary "process theology." #80270.

Wolfhart Pannenberg, by Don Olive. A profile of one of the younger European theologians. Pannenberg, whose creative thought challenges prevailing concepts, seeks to break out of the closed discipline approach typical of many theologians. #80251.

Sören Kierkegaard, by Elmer H. Duncan. Highlights of the life and important works of the great thinker who influenced Barth, Bultmann, Tillich, Brunner, Niebuhr. Expositions of his key ideas, explanations of his obscure terminology, and insights into his reactions to Hegel, Kant, Feuerbach, and others. #80463.

Martin Buber, by Stephen M. Panko. The leading spokesman of 20th-century Judaism whose thought has influenced most of the principal Christian thinkers. Includes study of his I-Thou concept, which has made such a profound impact on modern theology. #80470.